To Fiona
Many Thanks
For All The Support

An Abundance of Frogs

Further pieces written in the company of The Inkslingers Writers Group

Harry Browne

Acknowledgement

With grateful appreciation to
Rebeca Georgeta Bighiu
For her stunning cover Illustration

DEDICATION

Dedicated to my ten grandchildren, too numerous to mention by name.

All of you are a source of joy and pride for me. Thank you all.

Copyright © 2019 Harry Browne

InkSplinters Press

ISBN: 9781695781153

All rights reserved. No part of this publication may be reproduced, distributed, or transmitted in any form or by any means, including photocopying, recording, or other electronic or mechanical methods, without the written permission of the authors, except in the case of brief quotations embodied in critical reviews and certain other non-commercial uses permitted in copyright law.

Contents

Liquorice all sorts 13

Push Me 14

Studio Boat 16

Bottled 18

Bottled Up 19

Motorbikes 20

The Ravelled Sleeve 25

A goldfinch and a small cat. 26

Anthologitis* 28

Devil's Bargain 32

The Formal Jacket 34

Were Weyer Yis 36

Wolves 38

The brightest sunflower 39

Baby Shoes 41

Winter's Tale 42

Saving Hay 44

Multitasking 46

Saturnalia 48

The Box 50

The purple overcoat. 52

The Mouth of Time 53

The Prodigal Son 55

Lazyboy	57
The art of plamossin'	59
The Cup of Ambition	61
Lady in Red	63
Recipe for Disaster	65
Stuck in a Lift	67
Austerity	69
Fire Breathing	71
An Alien Concept	73
The Book Chair	75
Perilous Habit	77
Flying Anteater	79
Eighteenth Birthday	81
The Fourth Wall	83
Making Tracks	85
Technicolour Cake	87
Stone cushion	89
Best Laid Plans	91
Spelling Bee	93
Peasouper	96
Plane Companions	98
Every dog has his day.	100
Alice and the Cheshire Cat	102
Lethal Mix	104

True Love's Diamond 106

Rose of Tralee 108

Job Offer 110

Valkyrie 112

Vive la Resistance 114

Hound of Hell 116

Jimmy Choo's 118

An Antique Chair 120

Loser 122

Tough Love 124

Rock'n'Roll to me and Billy Joel 126

Accidental Arsonist 128

Airy Castles 129

Pearly Gates 131

Rabbit Hole 133

Snow White 136

Face Time 138

Paddy Paragon 140

Glendalough 142

Duvet Day 144

Hidden Treasure 146

The Bank Managers Dilemma 148

Puncture 150

A telephone call 152

Philosophical Musings 154

She Reaps a Cruel Revenge 156

Baked Treat.. 158

Irises by the Pond 160

Cloak and Dagger... 162

She Was Only Sixteen 164

Unrequited Love 166

Time Flies.. 168

Property of the State.. 170

Confounded Ambition 172

Crushed 174

Literati... 176

Opposition 178

Rosinante.. 180

Chaos in Government.. 182

Martian Volleyball.. 184

Mother Love... 186

Championship Ambitions 188

Vain Attempt.. 190

Dubious Alliances... 192

Topsy Turvey House 194

Wish in one Hand... 196

Control Issues... 198

Christmas Cheer 200

Fireman Sam	202
Wedding Cake	204
Rockfall	206
Tiger in a Bubble	208
Seen and Not Heard	210
Scaredy Monster	212
Back in The Day	214
Stop and think!	216
Sherwood	218
Christmas Shopping	220
Family Argument	222
Wild Ambition	224
Bees Knees	226
Hells Bells	228
A Fishy Tale	230
Ovine Golfer	232
Bum Gig	233
Aces High	235
Working Girl?	237
Talebearer	239
Monopoly Money	241
Pugilism	243
At the Swimming Pool	245
Dictator	247

Sing for your Supper	249
Shaggy Dog Story	251
Superbug	253
Pirate Woes	255
Argonauts at Sea	256
Kidnapped	259
Heroes for a Day	261
Euromillions	263
Loves Labour Lost	265
Conflict Resolution	267
Filthy Lucre	269
Cockalorum	271
Lost and Wandering	273
Capricious Nature	275
Poets and Lesser Mortals	277
Great Expectations	279
Civil Obedience	281
Parenting	283
Razorbill	285
Dreamtime	287
Bear Faced Cheek	289
Kidnapped	291
Clocks	293
Disappointment	295

Don't Open It!	297
Traffic Chaos	299
Doggone	301
Dream killer	303
Broccoli House	305
Travelling Hazards	307
Arachnophobia	309
Cruella de Ville	311
Bravery or Temerity?	313
Performance Anxiety	315
Childhoods End	317
A New Beginning	319
Patrick Puffin	321
Bucking Bronco	323
Book Burning	325
Prompt Prompts	326
Laced Up	328
Hyacinths and Roses	330
Plain Sailing	332
Oh lucky Man	334
Lies, Damn Lies.	336
Trains, Planes and a Leprechaun	338
Christmas Cheer	340

Liquorice all sorts

Harry tasted the item, which was in the bag, it had a powdery, sugary feeling to it and smelt vaguely of distant childhood. He was not very fond of liquorice and in his youth, he had always chosen the non liquorice sweets from the assortment if there were any left.

Sweets of any type were of course always acceptable and in a real emergency liquorice was good enough if nothing else was available.

His older sister had gotten a present of a huge box of chocolates and placed them carefully on the highest shelf of the wardrobe, thinking that they would be out of harm's way.

Silly girl! Harry found them and took a few to bed with him. Next night he took a few more, and the night after another few. This went on for some period of time.

Eventually Freda, his sister found an occasion good enough to open the sweets. Imagine her horror when all she found in the box were the nutty type which nobody in their right mind would eat, all the others were gone!

For some peculiar reason suspicion immediately fell on Harry. This seemed to be his lot in life. No matter what bad thing happened in the house Harry's name seemed to be associated with it. This despite the fact that he was as likely to be innocent as not. Sadly, that was not the case in this instance, he found himself the focus of almost universal condemnation

Push Me

She took the knife in her right hand, drew it across the stone and then ran her left index finger up along the blade. It would have cut her had she not been very careful. It would have to do.

Moving forward with extreme care she pressed the block on the wall which announced in bold letters 'Push Me'

With a grinding sound the wall in front of her pivoted ponderously releasing a puff of stale, sickly sweet smelling air from within. Jenny gagged at the stench but advanced unhesitatingly into the dimly lit chamber, gesturing over her shoulder for her brother to wait outside.

"Give me a chance to check this out" she said "I've got the knife so it's best if I go first. I'll give you a call if the room is clear"

"Bloody woman thinks she's the ruler of the world. Stay there, come here, do this, do that. I've a good mind to just go off and leave her to whatever quare thing she finds in there" Patrick had just arrived at an age where he felt that the gender balance in his family was somewhat skewed.

"Still" he thought "she does have a record of finding good stuff in these mausoleums, and fair play to her she did bring the pig sticker with her. I wouldn't have thought of it myself. Anyway, that room smells, and it looks a bit creepy, maybe it's best leave the macho stuff to her for the present"

Standing there pondering his options he failed to notice, until it was too late, that the wall was silently pivoting shut.

"Sis" he shouted, rushing towards the swiftly narrowing gap "Sis, the door, get back here" Pulling his rucksack off his shoulder he jammed it in the fast narrowing gap, leaving a finger width crack in the jamb of the door.

Jenny's voice echoed hollowly out of the inner room "What did you do, you cretin. I take all the risks, leave you one lousy task, to watch the door and as soon as I turn my back you get me trapped in here. Get me out of here, right now or it will be the worse for you"

Patrick struggled mightily with the door, pushing and pulling it every which way but all to no avail "Sorry Sis" he panted "I can't manage to get a budge out of it. I'll have to go and get help"

"Go where and get help?" she demanded exasperated beyond measure "We're twenty miles up a remote mountain in the Hindu Kush and the nearest help is a three day trek away. I could be dead and eaten by the time you get back in six days. And that doesn't take into account that the local Sherpas warned us not to go fossicking up here by ourselves. Remember what the old head man said about evil spirits in these mountains"

As he studied the situation Patrick was struck by a brilliant thought "Why didn't I think of that before?" He muttered and he poked the 'Push Me' block.

Studio Boat

(Claude Monet 1874)

With her faded dress and worn shoes she knew she couldn't go; however, Claude Monet wasn't having any of that nonsense.

"If I restricted access to my studio boat to those who only wear formal dress, I'd have a very lonely voyage" he proclaimed in an encouraging voice "Come aboard please, we will only take a short cruise down the Seine this afternoon"

"But Monsieur" The young woman said "I've never been on a boat before. Won't it be bumpy, I'd hate to mess your lovely craft by being seasick"

"No problem my dear" Replied the artist, extending his paint stained hand to her "Come along, I'll make sure that the journey is tranquil"

As the small boat traversed the smooth waters of the river, Monet struck up a conversation with his new companion "I saw you walking on the towpath and I was struck by your native poise and grace of movement. I would dearly love to paint you, if you would allow it"

"Oh dear, my sainted mother warned me about men like you. I won't take off my clothes for you or any man on the pretext of being painted. My parents raised me right"

"I'm not that sort of painter" Said the artist in a pained voice "I normally do landscapes, but in your case, I would like to paint you just as you are, clothes and all"

"But Sir" She protested "I couldn't allow you to paint me in these clothes. They are much too shabby to go on canvas. I don't know much about painting, but I do know that ladies are always dressed in their finest. These poor rags are not fit for painting"

"I'll be the judge of that" smiled Monet "Just sit up at the front of the boat, that's right just so and I'll do a quick sketch of you and the river. I'll return to the picture later to finish it in oils. Meantime would you like a glass of white wine and some strawberries?"

Bottled

Sculpture *Acceptable Losses 1* By Thomas Doyle

This business of living in a bottle has its own up, and down, side. Weather is not a major problem as the season is always equable and benign. Sometimes though a little rain or even a snowstorm might be a welcome break from the tedium. Wishing for a snowstorm in my situation may not be wise as a larger person might decide to lift the bottle and shake it to create a storm of flakes as children's toys sometimes do. There is no evidence that such an action would generate the storm as there are no flakes on the ground but the shaking by itself could be catastrophic.

I wonder where my wife is. She really should be home by now. Oh, well I'll just have to make my own tea.

Is that someone knocking on the door?

Bottled Up

Sculpture - *Acceptable Losses 2* by Thomas Doyle

Living, as I do, on the edge of a precipice can be a daunting experience but the view is truly spectacular.

I bought this house eight years ago at the height of the boom and it is an inextricable part of my life now. It would be difficult if not impossible for me to leave it for several reasons. Chiefly the fact that some time ago my wife went out for a bottle of milk and has not been seen for about two years. She has a problem at the best of times with navigation and finding the front door presents a challenge even to those of us less directionally challenged.

I'm almost sure she went out by the back door, but she had, in recent times taken to leaving and entering by one of the windows.

Some of you may think that this is eccentric behaviour but, myself, I haven't been outside in something over six years. All the supplies, groceries, fuel and other essentials are delivered to the long downstairs window and paid for on the Internet, so why would anyone need to leave the cosy confines of such a beautiful house?

I am getting concerned about my wife's absence. She has never been away so long before; it is very unlike her

Motorbikes

There are men and there are women and then as an entirely separate subspecies that are motorcyclists. Consider their mode of transport, it can hardly be described as a vehicle, Collins English Dictionary describes a vehicle as "A machine such as a car, bus, or truck which has an engine and is used to carry people from place to place" Nowhere in this definition does the motorcycle fit, it's an outlier, a rebellious construct from its inception. It's inherently unstable, relying as it does, on two wheels rather than, like any decent vehicle, a stable four. To mangle George Orwell in Animal Farm, "Four wheels good, two wheels bad"

If you exit your car and leave it on the side of the road, in neutral and without handbrake, it will be very likely be in the same place when you return, unless you are foolish enough to leave it in the above condition on a hill, in which case you deserve all you get,

Try the same thing with a motorcycle, it will fall over causing damage, at the very least to its expensive paintwork and at worst to passing traffic if it falls the other way. Yes, yes, I hear the cries of the aforesaid bikers. "You have a kickstand to prevent that" but then it's not a true two wheeled contraption, it's a two wheeled contraption with a kickstand

One hesitates to describe the riders of such a contraption as being similarly unstable; though there are days

20

when one wonders. Picture the scene, it's a cold Sunday morning in early spring and all decent minded citizens are sound asleep in their comfortable beds when the tranquil neighbourhood silence is shattered by the racket of a high powered engine being revved to a screaming crescendo before the miscreant in the saddle puts the bike in gear and roars off down the road for his Sunday constitutional in the mountains.

Shortly afterwards he, or she, is joined by a horde of like minded individuals, dressed as extras from a Star Wars movie, Then in a cloud of noxious fumes and multidecibel exhaust cacophony they head off in an untidy column, occupying much more than their share of the road space, to cavort along the twisty highways and byways of Wicklow, causing anxiety and upset to any decent minded other road users, unfortunate enough to encounter them on their peregrinations.

Meanwhile as our gallant hero's struggle through pouring rain and freezing winds their neighbours back home are just rising and starting a hot breakfast, Which would you rather be?

It is an extraordinary thing, but no motorcyclist ever falls off their bike. Sometimes the bike "Goes out from under them" but it is never their fault. There may have been loose gravel, or ice patches, or oil on the roads, or even the "Fat bastard in the Mercedes'" causing the bike to "Go out from under them" but it's never due to pilot error.

Consider, if you will, the sad plight of the parents of one of these deranged people, The phone rings at the worst possible moment of the day or night,

"Hello, are you the parent of Paul Browne?" Instant palpitations Of the heart!

"Yes, who is this calling?"

"Its Sister Hynes, Vincent's Hospital, Your son has been injured in a motorcycle accident and he is in A&E"

"Dear God, how is he? Is it serious?"

*'I'm afraid I can't answer that. GDPR, you understand. You can come in anytime"

"Thank you"

Forty panic stricken minutes later, after a drive at reckless speed from out of town the distraught parent arrive in the A&E to find the victim lying, bloodstained and half naked on a trolley and in a semi coherent state.

"Dad, Ma, is that you? They cut my good Furygan jacket off, it's ruined"

"Not to worry Son, we'll get another one. What happened?"

"1 was at a track day in Mondello and I was out in front and going well hit a patch of loose debris on the track and the bike went from under me. I was winning Dad"

"Son, in order to win you, and the bike, have to cross the finish line together. Not as two separate incidents. Now go to sleep. We'll talk more tomorrow"

The next day he's excitedly talking about the new, bigger and vastly improved bike, which he intends to buy and the new Furygan gear which he will get to go with it and his distracted parents are shaking their heads in despair.

Years pass and he's now a professional motorcycle guru with a motorcycling wife and two small sons and the scars of several episodes of bikes "Going from under him" having emigrated to the far North West Any reasonable person his circumstances would be considering settling down and retiring the infernal contraption. Not so. I would refer you to paragraph five above. This is a bug which looks like it will cling to him until he shuffles off the mortal coil, hopefully at an advanced age and not because his bike "Goes, catastrophically, out from under him"

On pondering on the genesis of his aberration one might consider genetics. His paternal great grandfather, Maurice, was the proud owner of a small fleet buses in the early years of the 1900s. His father was raised on stories of Maurice and his sons in those halcyon days of free enterprise before the advent of CIE.

Stories told of races with competing bus companies driving recklessly out the Drumcondra Road in an effort to scoop up passengers before the rivals and arguments, sometimes leading to fisticuffs as to who had first rights to routes abounded. Those "Good Old Days" finally came to an end when, after couple of cases of arson involving their buses, the government of the day stepped in, nationalised the bus companies and founded Coras Iompar Eireann or CIE, and put a stop to their shenanigans, There might be something genetics thing.

It must 'be acknowledged that, whatever the opinion of the more stable members of the community, these outlaws appear to enjoy their difference. Without exception when questioned they wax lyrical as to the benefits motorcycling. A common theme amongst them is that whilst going by car is travelling, biking is a transcendental experience.

It's not by coincidence of the most famous books written about motor cycling is Robert M. Pirsig's and the Art of Motorcycle Maintenance.

Pirsig's thesis is that to truly experience quality one must both embrace apply it as best fits the requirements of the situation. According to Pirsig, such an approach would avoid a great deal of frustration and dissatisfaction common to modern life. It may be that, consciously or otherwise, our bikers be buying into this philosophy, thus indicating a possible explanation for their offbeat approach to life, the universe and everything, there may be something in this, but it seems to have escaped the more mundane of us in the general population.

To paraphrase our hero's Great-Grand-Mother, a country lady born on a tiny farm in the Wicklow mountains in the latter part of the nineteenth century "There's a little bit of sense in the wildest of us, and a little bit of wildness wisest of us, so as wild as I am, and as wise as you are, I'm as wise as you are as wild as I am"

So perhaps we can best tip our hats to the outlaws and acknowledge that room in the world for all of us.

(June Issue 2019 BikeBuyersGuide)

The Ravelled Sleeve

"Thinking slow and fast is easier said than done" Paddy said in a reflective tone. He did not get much of a response, in fact he got no comprehensible response, unless ga, ga could be classified as a response.

Mind you he wasn't really expecting much of a response, after all he was talking to his three week old grandchild as he paced the room in a vain attempt to persuade her to sleep.

His lady wife, known to one and all as 'my immediate superior' called from their bedroom "Have you wakened the child again, you old fool? Don't think you're fooling anybody that she wakened herself. Everybody knows well that with the slightest peep you're up and into her room in the hopes that you'll find her with her eyes half open"

"The child suffers from insomnia, that's all" Replied Paddy "It's not fair to ignore the little mite when all she needs is some stimulating conversation and sparkling wit. And who better to provide that than her doting grandfather?"

"Stimulation is it? The last thing the child needs at 4 o'clock in the morning is stimulation. Put her back into her cot and come back into bed before I send for the men in the white coats" snarled My immediate' and pulling the sheets up over her head she snuggled down with a muttered "Silly old fool"

Paddy continued with his soliloquy but even to his besotted eyes the baby was in a profound sleep, so he gently returned her to the cot, covered her with the Alice in Wonderland blanket and stole quietly, and obediently, back to bed.

A goldfinch and a small cat.

The very small cat called, somewhat unimaginatively, Felix, eyed the goldfinch which was perched just out of reach and singing its little heart out all unaware of the imminent peril which he represented.

"Noisy little sqwaker, isn't he" he muttered to himself. "I'll soon choke off his caterwauling if I can only get high enough up that tree. If he doesn't want to be eaten, he should keep his yap shut, or take it somewhere else" Felix tended to be very territorial about his back garden. to describe it as his back garden could be considered as a misnomer in some quarters, particularly from the perspective of the person who was burdened by a huge negative equity situation vis a vis the premises attached to the said back garden, but cats, as we all know operate in a different reality to other species, especially cash strapped and zero hour contract workers like the one under discussion here.

The goldfinch, Frankie by name, continued with his impromptu concert. He not unnaturally had a different agenda to Felix. His sole and only focus on this bright and sunny morning was to find a female of his species and have his wicked way with her. So far his quest was in vain as the availability of female goldfinches in the neighbourhood was peculiarly scarce, perhaps due to the depredations of our friend Felix.

Tiring of his thankless labours Frankie looked around and noticed, for the first time, the presence of the predatory feline hiding, unsuccessfully in the shrubbery. "No bloody wonder I'm not having any luck" He grumbled "The chicks will hardly be lining up for a bit of how's yer father while that ugly bastard is hanging around"

Changing his tune to a rallying call for assistance he was soon the centre of a large flock of assorted avians of varying shapes and sizes, prominent amongst them three large seagulls. One of the gulls approached Frankie and demanded "Hey shortass, what's the gig. I heard there was a call to have a go at a cat. I can't see anything only a scrawny little kitten, we gulls have a reputation to uphold, we can't be seen to stoop so low and to pick up so little. We were designed for bigger things" he squawked and with a tremendous flapping of wings he and his fellow gulls took off.

Frankie was somewhat put out by this desertion until he noticed a female of the appropriate species sidling up beside him "Hey big guy" She trilled in his earhole "Why don't we take off and find a quiet spot where we can be undisturbed, high enough that the bastard cat can't get at us and we can shit on him from a height?"

Anthologitis*

(The disease of the need to contribute to, or facilitate the assembly, collation and/or publication of anthologies)

Brendan Behan, writer of this parish was once asked why he took up the writer's pen as a profession, His reply was classic Brendan – "Because I suffered from Muradecrophobia, the disease of having to paint walls for a living"

Brendan was fortunate. At least the walls stood still while he was working on them. Dealing with a group of writers, of all styles and genres and levels of confidence can be compared to the task of minding frogs in a wheelbarrow. Nice Frogs, very capable Frogs, but with regard to discipline? The Augean Stables would be less taxing.

Back in 2013 I entered for The Novel Fair in The Irish Writers Centre on Parnell Square. Not surprisingly, as there were 350 other entrants, I didn't make the long list, never mind the short one. But I did find myself with a finished novel. Knowing several writers and being in their company in the Writers Centre I enquired widely as to how I might go about publishing my work. One successful author told me "I wouldn't mind the rejection slips; I have one wall of my bedroom papered in rejection slips"

I decided right there and then that that route was not for me. After some research I found Amazon's self publishing arm, CreateSpace, and I discovered my metier.

Self publishing on CreateSpace, now called Kindle Direct Publishing, is absurdly easy. Mind you, Maura Laverty had a famous recipe for roast duck, which started 'you must first catch your duck', So too, in order to self publish, you must first have a book! Ideally you should also have a cover for that book, a blurb, and a dedication. After that it's a doddle!

In order to deal with KDP you must first have an Amazon Account. This involves setting up the amount with Amazon and giving them details of your credit card number and also your IBAN and BIC numbers. Obviously, you will need to buy copies of your book from them, hence the credit card details, and also, as they will be selling your book on Kindle they must have your bank details in order to forward the loot to you.

This entire process is absolutely free up to the point when you want to buy author copies for yourself. These copies are produced at production cost plus postage and, depending on the cover price, decided by the author, come at a fraction of the sale price.

Many people have major reservations about trading over the internet with understandable issues regarding security, hacking etc. In order to mitigate these concerns the simple thing is to set up a separate, isolated bank account with a minimal amount lodged. Then when the time comes to buy books all that's needed is to deposit the amount required prior to purchasing. Also depending on how successful your book is on the Kindle sales you can sit back and watch the money roll in. Mind you, holding your breath waiting for sales may not be a good idea.

All the foregoing is the easy part. Putting together an anthology Involving fifty writers and one hundred and fifty pieces can be a daunting task. For many people the concept of a deadline is anathema. Some have a very flexible notion as to what midnight on 28th February means. We, in the Inkslingers have produced six anthologies in the past six years and despite the collator's dictatorial insistence that a deadline is a deadline this simple concept seems to escape some. There is the inevitable plea that "I have just a few hours more work to do on it. Can I please have an extension?" which still raises its ugly head after all the years.

In putting together the anthology our rules are few and simple. Pieces contributed will be included unedited and as supplied. The collator takes no responsibility for the content, unless it's scurrilous, defamatory, libellous or just plain offensive. No editorial oversight will be applied, and errors of typesetting, syntax or grammar are the author's responsibility alone. There is a word count limit, but it tends to be flexible as the pieces offered vary widely in length, from five line Haikus to multi page fully dramatized plays.

Ideally, especially if you are a poet, poets tend to be picky about how the piece looks on the page, you should first decide on the page size, margins and page count as early in the process as possible. If you submit your masterpiece on an A4 format KDP will print it as best it fits the finished book, not always ideal. Therefore, try setting up your page size and do your typing on that size from the outset.

Adding illustrations is as simple as inserting them wherever and whenever it suits you, remember that if you choose a black and white finish to your magnum opus the pictures, whether shown in colour or otherwise will be printed in black and white. You can always choose to have your book printed in full colour but that tends to be more expensive. The illustrations on the digital, Kindle, copy appear in whatever colour you have them in the original text.

Kindle will offer you a free ISBN number or you can purchase one yourself on the internet, though why you would do that is not clear to us.

Also offered is a free series of covers which you can automatically apply, again free of charge. There is a full, professional service offered of everything from editing to cover design and everything in between at a range of charges which is completely optional.

Finally, the vexed question as to sales and distribution. First things first, set a price which will make it worthwhile to equate to the amount of effort you have put into the writing, rewriting, editing and just plain soul searching to get it to this point, adding in the purchase price of the books and the postage.

Secondly, do, by all means have a book launch. It's a huge ego boost to have a group around you telling you how clever you are and asking your advice on how to go about the process. And you will not get a better opportunity to put the squeeze on your relations, friends, godmothers, godfathers, work colleagues and total strangers, in one place and at one time to sell them your pride and joy.

Do be careful as to the number of books you buy in anticipation of the launch. Even at $5.00 each if you buy 100 it works out at €450.00. Add the room rent and a few bottles of cheap wine and pretty soon you're into significant figures. Buy less rather than more. You can always have a second run.

After that you are into hard work territory. John Locke has written a book which tells you in detail how to market your digital books. You can find it on Kindle at "John Locke How I sold 1 million eBooks in five months" it costs a couple of euros and gives an in depth run down on how to sell eBooks. Don't get me wrong, it's hard work. Smashwords.com have good, free, eBooks on Marketing and also style guides. Worth checking out. Kindle also offer online advice on how to put together sales campaigns online. The campaign itself will only charge when books are sold.

Regarding hard copy books. Pretty much all independent booksellers will accept copies on a sale or return basis. Some of the chains will as well but they must have an ISBN number. This is also hard work.

Remember, very, very few people make a living out of selling books, either self published or through conventional publishing houses.

That said, get up and go. Just do it. You'll be delighted.

Devil's Bargain

(Monolith Yosemite National Park – Ansel Adams c1927)

"Someday Jamie, when you're grown up, all this will be yours" The smartly dressed being with the red skin and forked tail said, pointing out at the wide vista of barren rock and ice spread out as far as the eye could see.

"Dear God" replied Jamie "I didn't sign away my immortal soul for a load of frozen and broken rock. When I entered into a deal with you, I expected to be supreme ruler of all that I surveyed. I expected something a bit more welcoming than this frozen version of a Viking hell than what you're offering me now"

"Jamie, Jamie, Jamie" Chided the supreme evil "let's not bring him into this. Surely, you've heard the old saying that when you sup with the devil you should bring a long spoon? I am offering you sole rule over all that you survey. You didn't specify just what you wanted to survey. You should have been more discriminating over what you signed, especially with me. I have almost every single lawyer and law maker who ever existed in my thrall in the bottom pit of hell. If anyone can draw up a contract in their own favour, it's me and my souls in torment. You just never had a chance once you started to lust after power and influence"

32

"Well I want to challenge the contract. I wasn't in possession of all the facts when I signed up. There were several things that, in law, you should have made me aware of, but you told me absolutely nothing. I was bamboozled" Jamie whined.

With a snap of his fingers and a puff of red smoke Old Nick produced a stack of paper as thick as a New York telephone directory and thrust it under Jamie's nose "Look here fool, this is the contract we signed, in multiplicate, in the presence of witnesses. You can't claim that you didn't read it. I told you on several occasions to read it before signing but you thought you'd never get your hands on your new dominion, you figured you knew better. Well now comes your comeuppance"

"This is worse than the bloody leaving cert. I'll just turn the mountain into a ski resort and soldier on with it and you can have the begrudgers" Snarled Jamie.

The Formal Jacket

The man in the formal jacket was somewhat annoyed, in fact he was severely pissed off. He had set out that morning in high good humour to meet his girlfriend in the city centre, dressed not only in his formal jacket but wearing his brand new scarlet waistcoat and matching bow tie, together with has his cool shirt with French cuffs and cuff links which were only to die for. Sadly, his plans were doomed to disappointment.

In the first place she was late, as usual, but unusually when he finally spied her approaching, she was draped on the arm of a young Adonis with wavy blonde hair, shiny shoes and a Hilfiger sweater thrown carelessly over his shoulders.

"Hi, Peter," she said "have you met Carlos?"

"No" said Peter, "I don't believe I have"

"Oh, sorry" Maria said "This is Carlos, my husband, he's just back from a long trip to the Amazon jungles. You know, protecting the wildlife and saving the planet and such"

Peter was a little taken aback by this unexpected turn of events, he had been seeing Maria for several months and their relationship was so intense that he had just the day before bought a ring with the intention of popping the question today! He was a little older than Maria, but he was really of the opinion that they had something special going together.

"You never told me you were married" he whinged.

"You never asked" she replied

"It just never came up" said our gallant hero.

"Well if it's a problem just say so, I was just going to suggest a threesome, but if that's awkward for you we'll give it a miss"

"A threesome" said Peter "but where will we go?"

"I was thinking we could go to the Zoo and feed the monkeys" she replied. "Carlos knows all about monkeys after his time in the Amazon"

Peter looked at her in astonishment. He had been thinking of a totally different type of threesome.

Now in a different frame of mind from his early morning high spirits, Peter said "no thanks" and stormed off in a huff.

Going home to his Mammy he demanded to know just what is wrong with all the women he meets. They are either married, in unique relationships with gay men, or women, or confirmed man haters.

"where are all the nice women?" he cried!

"Sadly, son" she said, "I'm the last nice woman on Earth"

Were Weyer Yis

"Howayizz" says Jacinta

"Im' not talkin' to youse" he says "Where weyer yis wen I woz in de slammer?'

"Were d'ja tink I woz" she screeches "I woz a' home mindin' them li'lle gets of yours. You go' yerself caugh' an banged up, leavin' me wi' all the kids and the bleedin' bills. An then ye have the gall to shou' a' me abou' you bein inside.

Jayze, I could do wi' a couple of munce in the Joy meself, just for a break like" She was obviously at the end of her tether.

"It's nor all beer an' skittles inside ya know" He tried sweet reason with her. It didn't work before his spell inside and he was not too surprised to find it equally unsuccessful now.

"Beer an' skittles is i', I'll give you beer an skittles" brandishing a frying pan she rushed at him with a homicidal look on her face.

"Now doll" If reason failed perhaps sweet talk might. "Wy don' we go down the boozer an' gerra couple pints inta us an' I'll try ta tink up some way of makin' ir up ta ye"

"An who d'ya tink is goin' ta mind the ankle biters. Me poor Ma is moidered wi' tryin' ta keep an eye on them wen I has ta go ta me cleanin' job, so she's not willin'"

"I'll ask me sister" He said

"Yer sister? thas a good wan. She was took for stree' walkin' in de Gloucester Dimond las ni'. She's in the wimmin's in the Joy cause she hasn't go' bail"

"Jaysus Christ" He said "A poor workin' man can't gerra break in this God forsaken country. It's bad enough the're cuttin' the social and the mickey money bu' putting' workin' gerils in jail is the last straw. I be' they didn pu the John in clink."

Wolves

Night fell and again he dreamt of Wolves. Wolves with glaring red eyes and sharp, slavering teeth.

Teeth were also another strong motif in his nightmares, Dracula style teeth, long sharp and pointed and discoloured by blood. The blood of innocent men, women and children who had done nothing to deserve their bizarre fate.

Fate had decreed that he suffer, nightly, for the sins of his distant ancestors who had roamed the Carpathian mountains, the seat of their families holdings which had been theirs for uncounted centuries until the rise of communism, which had stolen their land and outlawed their ancestral privilege.

Privilege, he mused carried a double burden, on the one hand the thrill of the chase and the dark pleasure of the draughts of red living blood at the end. On the other hand, the duty of care to their tenants, who were in a very real sense their flock. They must be cared for and nourished in order that a continuous supply of the liquor of life should be abundantly available as and when a need arose.

Once more night fell and again, he dreamt of Wolves.

The brightest sunflower

As a small child I was seriously scared of sunflowers. In the first place, they were invariably much taller than me and their heads were bigger than mine. This is not an inconsiderable issue for a small boy.

Smaller flowers can be trampled underfoot and have their blooms pulled and strewn around the garden. But flowers too tall to reach even at full stretch are a challenge which no normal small boy should be faced with.

The second characteristic of sunflowers is that they turn and watch you as you play near them. The movement of their heads is not perceptible because they are sneaky, but it is an undeniable fact the if they are looking one way at a given time, an hour later they have changed their aspect so that no matter where you go to wreak havoc they have you in their sights. Furthermore, I was, and remain to this day, convinced that they also ratted me out to my parents when I misbehaved, which was a very frequent occurrence.

My sainted aunt Betty (horrible old dragon as she is) always professed to love sunflowers. I never believed her as to my certain knowledge, she loved nothing and nobody.

She used to crow with false delight when she saw the sunflowers in our garden and cry out "Oh how I love your sunflowers Sheila" (Lying old bitch, she only said this to make me feel small. As if I wasn't small enough already." The best thing about sunflowers is their lovely bright, shining faces" was another of her favourite chants.

She got her comeuppance in the end though. One day whilst I was hiding in the dense shrubbery at the end of the garden watching, I saw the Old Dragon traipsing through the garden handing out lavish amounts of criticism to my dear mother. "Sheila Dear" she said "Don't you think that those delphiniums would be better over the other side, you've cut the grass too close again. I've told you repeatedly, Sheila, you mustn't over cut the grass".

Entering the dreaded sunflower patch, she tripped over a stray root, fell awkwardly and, to my intense delight, broke her neck and went to her unlamented and overdue reward.

When asked in later years what she had died from, my mother would say, with a wry smile "She died from the brightest sunflower of all"

Baby Shoes

The ad was placed prominently on the local supermarket notice board "For Sale, Baby Shoes, Never Worn".

"Ahh, that's very sad" Jenny said. She's a very kind person, always ready to help stray, or is it lame, dogs over stiles and stuff. This has gotten her into trouble on many occasions, not the least when she put a dog among a herd of prize merino lambs on McDonnell's farm. The resulting carnage didn't make a pretty sight as it turned out that the dog in question was not as lame as Jenny had thought.

"Why sad" Jim queried "It's not necessarily all bad, they might have been an unwanted present or bought too small for an oversized baby. There's no reason to assume disastrous reasons for selling shoes you know".

"No, I'm sure there's a tragedy behind this ad" Jenny's caring instincts were in full arousal mode. "I have a picture of a distraught mother having lost a baby for whom she had lovingly knitted tiny baby shoes for which there was no need in the end".

"Or it might be a shoe factory selling last year's lines. Remember the winter coat you got at Jimmy Hourihan's a couple of years ago. That was a real bargain, and it had never been worn before you bought it". Jim tended to wax philosophical on occasion.

"Do these melons look ripe to you" He asked as they passed on about their grocery shopping.

Winter's Tale

"Jeez" he said as his long suffering wife pulled off his high, black boots "This damn job gets harder every year"

"Worse than usual, was it?" She queried sympathetically.

"Nah, I wouldn't go so far as that" He sighed "It's just that I'm not getting any younger and getting around to five billion houses in one evening is becoming a major drag. It wouldn't be so bad if you could go in the front door, like any normal person, but shimmying down chimneys at my stage of life gets old mighty fast. And then there's the dogs, why do dogs always have to raise a racket? I suppose they can't be blamed for being a little touchy about the unconventional mode of entry, but when they try to gnaw your leg off it's not great craic"

"And what about the dissatisfied customers. I never heard such a flood of foul mouthed vituperation as I got from that ill mannered brat in number 47 Glasnevin avenue. He apparently wanted a transformer truck or six, but the idiot elf, Gandalf, in despatch, wrapped a full size doll, dressed in a pink frilly tutu and addressed it to him. I can assure you he was less than impressed.

We'll soon have to do something about Gandalf, he gets more gaga by the day. Last week on the harnessing trials, he put poor Randolph into the shafts of the snow vehicle facing backwards. That wouldn't have been the end of the world, but he'd already put Prince in right way round and with Randolph heading west and Prince going east there was an almighty bust up and Randolph missed the trip this year because he was recuperating in the animal Hospital"

"Where's that idle young Kris? He was supposed to be waiting to unyoke the snow vehicle when I got back, but, as usual, when there's a bit of work to be done he's away off hiding somewhere, probably with his nose stuck in a book"

"Now Nicholas" Brunilda scolded "Don't be too hard on the boy, he's only forty five years old, after all, and he's not fond of dealing with the snow vehicle pulling animals. One of them bit him on the arse yesterday when he was forking hay into her stall and he's having a lie-in this morning"

"If that good for nothing layabout thinks he's going to inherit the business from me just on the basis that he's my son, then he has another think coming. I didn't spend the last three hundred years building up this gig and selling my soul to commercial interests to have it run into the ground by a useless ne'er do well like him. I'd rather leave it to Gandalf, at least he likes kids".

"I won't hear you bad mouthing the lad like that". Brunilda was well on her high horse now. "He's your own flesh and blood and it's your fault he's as feckless as he is. You won't give him any responsibility or authority. No wonder he doesn't do what you want"

"Well he can take the whole bloody lot on next year; I'm going to spend the months of December and January in the Bahamas and put my feet up. So There"

Saving Hay

("Origins and Uses of Round Towers" Gareth Kennedy)

When I was a child me and my siblings, some of them anyway, used to be deposited on my mother's unfortunate Uncle Tom on his tiny farm in Corragh in County Wicklow, about as far back in the mountains as you can get. There we would spend a couple of months in a thatched cottage with no electricity, no running water, no radio, and the nearest shop was in Hollywood, some five miles away.

My abiding memories of those sojourns are of endless days of brilliant sunshine with milking cows, chasing sheep, skinny dipping in the local stream, which in these latter years seems to be much smaller than it used to be, and making hay.

Gareth Kennedy's "Origins and Uses of Round Towers" reminds me of our contribution to the hay making and saving process. We were tasked with the job of bringing tin cans, called Tinnys filled with extremely strong milky tea to the men who were working in the fields. This along with doorsteps of fresh baked soda bread was the staple fare for their break.

After the hay had been cut and left to dry over a number of days it needed to be saved. This involved collecting it up and piling it into cocks for later transport into the barn where it was stored for the winter cattle feed.

The building of these cocks of hay was a skilled operation and in order for them to be protected from being blown away in the wind, ropes were twisted from wisps of hay and thrown over the hay cocks with stones hanging from their ends to weight them down.

Our idea of fun was to climb on the hay cocks and slide down like a dry run at tobogganing. Needless to remark this didn't help the integrity of the hay cocks and was a practice much frowned upon by the grand Uncle Tom.

Looking at Gareth Kennedy's construction I can only assume that he would probably not appreciate our approach to his work either.

Multitasking

Multitasking, an activity considered by some to be exclusively a female art, is by its very nature an antisocial activity. The very activity of multitasking demands that the multitasker is not paying exclusive attention to either any specific task, or to any unfortunate who may be attempting to communicate with her, or him, who shall be known henceforth as MT for the sake of brevity.

The end result of which antisocial activity is that MT will, in the words of the old saying inevitably fall between two, or possibly more, stools.

One of the very few excuses for this nasty activity is the position of drummer in a musical group. Some experts will allege that the drummer is not, in fact a musician within the accepted meaning of that term, but such an allegation is, on the face of it an outrageous claim and does not deserve to be repudiated.

Any drummer worth their salt can play a tarradiddle with his, or her, left hand, the kettle drum with the right hand, the big bass with the right foot all whilst sounding the cymbals with the remaining left lower appendage. This, then is carrying the art of multitasking to the ultimate. I fact, some drummers can also sing whilst doing the aforementioned, amazing as that may seem.

Others may claim that they are engaging in multitasking, but this is arrant nonsense. They are merely behaving extremely badly. They cannot be bothered to pay attention to whatever is happening around and prefer to surround themselves with a plethora of their own selfish interest with scant regard for others.

Therefore, with the honourable exception of the previously mentioned drummers I strongly recommend that multitasking be barred from all social activities with immediate effect and it is my intention to have a private member's bill raised in the Dáil with this object in mind.

Given the abysmal record of policing the enormous number of laws promulgated by that august body I will propose that the policing of this heinous crime be left in the hands of private citizens. Any public spirited person who comes upon one of the despicable MTs will be entitled to administer as many slaps to the back of their heads as is necessary to force them to desist immediately.

Failure to respond would, under the new law, to be called The Punishment For Multitasking Law, will entitle the aforementioned public spirited person to resort to the liberal application of the wooden spoon.

Saturnalia

Four culture vultures hovered over the dead body of James Joyce. "I dunno, he looks a bit on the over ripe side to me" Said Cedric "What do you guys think?"

Cardew, ever ready to be as disagreeable as possible shouted "Poor old Shakespeare was a lot riper and it didn't stop you from chomping down on him. Personally, I find that all writers, no matter how young or old are a little bit dry and dusty for my taste"

Cormac, attempting to pour oil on troubled waters as was usual for him temporised "Oh, surely not all writers, that Cecilia Ahern now, I can't wait til she pops her clogs, she strikes me as a very tender morsel"

The chief of the clutch, Columbanus broke in "Enough of this talk. if you don't like what's on offer, Cedric, you can join another flock of carrion eaters, the very name of our species should be enough to give you a clue as to what might be on the dinner menu at any one time.

Writers as every educated person knows, don't die young, they linger on whinging pathetically about the magnum opus which they somehow never got to write and moulder away until finally the grim reaper arrives to put them and their audience out of their misery, whereupon their books hit the

48

best seller list and make their agents and publishers loads and loads of cash. Too late unfortunately to do the original writer any good.

The end result is that the meat tends to be dried up and stringy and the bones are calcified and chalky"

As they haggled over the mangled remains of the famous scribe a dragonfly flittered past "Hey guys" He cried in a tiny piping voice "Are yis goin to the saturnalia tonight? There'll be wine, women and song so there will

"Saturnalia?" Queried Cedric "What's that, is it some sort of church festival or something?

Denis, the Dragonfly snorted "I don't really think that church festival accurately fits the description. No, it's Saturday night tonight, time for the Roman feast of Saturnalia, a night of unbridled licentiousness and lust where we can all eat drink and be merry until the dawn breaks tomorrow"

Sadly, Columbanus shook his bald head and shrugged his drooping shoulders "Culture Vultures don't indulge in that class of carry on" He said "Ours is a melancholy duty and getting involved in stuff like that would completely spoil our image. However, if you would like a bite of James Joyce's arse, be my guest"

The Box

This box, to spite its small size, represents a chapter in our family history. The story, at least as far as I have been told, goes something like this. In the turmoil that was the last days of the British empire in Dublin one of the events was a raid on a bank in town and as luck, or whatever, would have it, our grandfather one Maurice Browne was on the premises at the time and managed to help himself to a few fists full of gold sovereigns which he subsequently held in this tin box. Careful inspection of the lid of this box will reveal my grandads name, which only goes to prove the truth of what I am saying.

Looking inside however you will not find any of the aforementioned sovereigns as they are well and truly spent, and not by me I hasten to add. What you will find in there is of considerable interest to me, however.

There are tokens which were minted for the skinners guild and come from a long way back in our history, one of our ancestors was a wealthy man and a leading light in the Skinners guild. It would appear that these pieces of metal have the highest monetary value of the lot. But what is of more value to me is the epaulet badges made of some soft gold coloured metal; these come from the uniform of a Dublin Corporation contract inspector. Maurice occupied that august position as his profession, a position which my father, his son, was also to occupy to spite Maurice's opposition. Maurice was a strange man in his way and had an iron control over his children all but two of whom pre decided him.

My own father being a notable exception. One of his crimes being that he got married, and for Maurice that was a no-no as it would inevitably lead to a loss of power once a new family was formed.

Another of his sons, named Harry as it happens, owned and ran one of Dublin's first bus companies. Whether or not the seed capital came through this box is anyone's guess at this stage. Somehow, I would like to think that it did.

The story goes that when his house was raided by the dreaded black and tans, Maurice sat on this tin (with the sovereigns inside) until they had removed themselves from his house. He was well able to maintain his composure throughout the proceedings, which was no mean feat, as he was sitting on more than the value of the entire house and its contents and once he could maintain his seat, he was quite prepared for them to do their worst.

On the death of my aunt, and Maurice's last remaining offspring, it fell to my brother Brian to administer her estate and among her papers was this small cash box just as you see it now. The keys were presumed to be for the family vault in Glasnevin. This vault is situated in the area known as the O'Connell circle which at the time of its inception was designed to house the great man himself. Apparently, it was a way for the new cemetery to attract the fashionable classes to "occupy", the new cemetery as it wear.

Alas the current contents of the box are hardly worth a fraction of what was once held there, if the family tradition is to be believed. However, it is perhaps just as well that the value is not excessive as the temptation to sell might otherwise be too great

The purple overcoat.

My sainted mother was an accomplished seamstress. Formal gowns, made for dress dances, the predecessor of today's Debs, were made for my sisters, cousins, female neighbours and friends.

My childhood home was continuously full of semi dressed young women and the whir of the foot operated sewing machine.

This was not a money making enterprise. As far as I am aware, she never got any payment for her efforts, the gratitude of the multitude of girls was more than enough return for her work.

This philanthropic work was all well and good until she decided to turn her hand to making a winter overcoat for me.

The material chosen for this ill conceived venture was a particularly virulent purple tweed mixture, woven at the witching hour by a blind and malevolent pixie who was undergoing a deep period of loathing for all man and pixie kind.

My maternal uncle Jack, always ready with the unkindest cut of all, upon being shown this misbegotten garment immediately christened it The Dogbox, a name which clung on like a bad smell.

It was named so because it was made without a pattern and hung from my scrawny shoulders like a reprimand to all dressmakers everywhere. It was, as the saying goes "Straight down and no nonsense".

Being, as I am, a caring and considerate individual I wore the atrocious garment for years afterwards, in order to spare my mother's feelings. It was, as might be expected, made with growing room built in.

I have in my lifetime lost many things, shoes, socks, and on one memorable occasion my schoolbag, which fell into the Royal Canal, but the damn coat stuck to me like a bad conscience.

In my infrequent nightmares that coat haunts me still.

The Mouth of Time

The temptation was irresistible. Here he was, an intrepid explorer faced with an honest to God, genuine, one hundred carat Black Hole. Did he have the bottle to continue? The mouth of time sucked at him like an arid sponge exposed to an Irish summer day.

To the best of his knowledge nobody had ever gone through a black hole before, or if they had they didn't return to brag about it.

Could he ever face himself again if he passed on this chance?

"Oh what the hell, Hitler took a chance" he mused as he strode confidently forward.

Perhaps the reference to Hitler was ill advised because he suddenly found himself in the middle of a large assembly of people dressed in brown shirts all of whom seemed to be in the process of strangling themselves by screaming at the top of their lungs a phrase which sounded awfully like "Seig Heil" and holding their arms erect in a clenched fist salute.

The Prodigal Son

"You did what?" Shouted the stay at home lad, "This toe rag nearly beggars the family, heads off whoring around the Arabian Peninsula, loses all his money on wine women and gambling. Not content with that but when he's finally fallen to his predestined position of swine herd he ups and comes home.

And what is your response, you kill the fatted calf, we've been saving that blasted animal for years now, in fact it must be the fatted ancestor by now, anyway, he comes home destitute and you throw him the party to end all parties. You must be going gaga"

"Now son, that's no way to be going on about your aged Father. You know he's my youngest son and he was the apple of your Mother's eye when he was little God rest her sainted soul. All the time he was gone I dreamt about him coming home and now, by the Grace of God, here he is. It's a miracle, so it is"

"Miracle is it? More like a disaster, you can't be so far gone in your dotage as to think he'll stay home. Oh no, give him a couple of months to get you twisted around his little finger and he'll be off gallivanting hither thither and yon again and this time he'll really bankrupt us.

Well I for one won't stand for it. It's my turn now, so cough up my share of the inheritance and I'll be off myself. That waster is not the only one in this family with a special talent for going through wads of cash. The only reason I haven't done it so far is because you've got a dead man's grip on the purse strings. So out with it, get the keys to the treasury and let's go"

"OK my son, but can I go with you?"

Lazyboy

(The prompt for this was: 'A Letter from one of your favourite pieces of furniture')

Dear John,

You will no doubt be surprised to receive this letter. Not only because it's from your trusty Lazyboy, but also, I bet you never knew I could read and write too.

See now, most people, yourself included, think that furniture is just dumb stuff, which is only good for filling rooms but, self evidently that's just wrong. I mean, if I was just a convenient place for you to plant your hairy arse when you come home from work would you be reading this letter right now? Not by a long chalk, you wouldn't.

To give the devil his due, you're not the worst in the "Furniture owning stakes" though that's an example of unparalleled arrogance in itself. I mean, who gave you the right to be the owner of a handsome piece like myself. What ever happened to banning slavery and universal suffrage and all that guff. I mean we're all human after all, in some sense anyway.

But I got fed up with the way I've been treated lately in this house. It was alright up until recently when you started smoking that wacky baccy stuff and inviting strangers into the gaff, why only last week you had that slapper in with the yappy rat dog that scratched my upholstery and pissed on my front leg.

But it all came to a head when the spinning orb, the semi translucent man and the quare looking angel came on the scene. I mean, enough is enough. What's a decent chesterfield lazy boy to think?

I have standards to maintain, you know. I come from a long, illustrious line of hand carved, high end furniture; I'll have you know.

Now there's no point in traipsing around all the antique shops looking for me. Even if I was in one of those places, I wouldn't stoop so low as to crawl back when you'd come looking. Actually, I've got a cushy gig in Aras An Uactharain, the president's place in the park, you know. The little fella up in the park is a little bit short arsed and he needed a chair that would allow him to sit down and place his feet on the floor at the same time and my unique characteristics fitted the bill exactly.

So, you can go away off with yourself, so you can.

Yours in amity,

The old armchair.

The art of plamossin'

"You must be jokin" Squawked the Kingfisher, "You're no more a Bird of Paradise than me uncle is me aunt. Would you ever give over your plamossin' and get real"

"Ah don't be too hard on him" chirped the Sparrow "If we all made ourselves, we'd be brilliant. Real Birds of Paradise live in tropical countries, if one of them were here they'd stand out like a whore in a cathedral. So, if our friend the ugly crow wants to claim that he's something he's most emphatically not, who are we to rain on his parade. Self deception is not a bad thing in all cases"

"Who're you callin' an ugly crow?" Demanded the self styled Bird of Paradise, "One more chirp outta you an' you'll find yourself scattered over the three adjacent counties. Crows are the top of the avian food chain, so they are" And tucking his head under his wing he went into a sulk.

Jimmy, who had been enjoying his al fresco breakfast looked on with open mouthed amazement at this confabulation of birdies. Turning to his long suffering other half he said, "I didn't know birds could talk, did you?"

"Of course birds can talk" She who must be obeyed snapped waspishly, she was a bit teed off with Jimmy this morning, this was the third time this week he'd made exactly the same comment and it tended to get a bit old after several repetitions. "Ravens do it if you split their tongues, or so my mother tells me, and parrots do it all the time"

"But that's not exactly talking" said an affronted Jimmy "They're only repeating the sounds they've heard if it's repeated often enough. This lot are having an extended conversation and

I don't know about you, but I can understand them. That's a bit strange no matter how you look at it"

"That's because you've a bird brain" snapped his immediate superior, gathering up the crockery and storming off into the kitchen.

"Well' muttered Jimmy, careful that his beloved not hear him "A bird in your head is worth much more than one in the bush anyway!"

(Plamossin' – Sweettalking)

The Cup of Ambition

Coffee is a language in itself.
— Jackie Chan

Every morning it was the same thing for Martin Hedges. He'd put on a pot of coffee and get dressed while he waited for the coffee to brew, but today things would be different....

In the first place he had no coffee in the house, no milk, no sugar, no doughnuts. In point of fact, the cupboard was as bare as a baboon's arse. To compound his confusion even further, he had no money to buy the aforesaid victuals.

For most of us this would not present a catastrophe, but Martin was not only economically challenged but fraternally bereft also. He had no mother, no father, no brothers, no sisters. Not to put too fine a tooth in it but poor Martin did not have one soul in the whole world who gave a tuppeny damn if he never tasted coffee again. He was friendless, childless, motherless, fatherless and even, one might go so far as to say, all alone in the world.

Who's to say which one of us, finding ourselves in Martin's dilemma might just have curled up in bed, pulled the covers over our heads and given way to howling despondency.

But not Martin Hedges. This man was made of sterner stuff than is common. Shrugging his shoulders and heaving one silent sigh, he headed off out into the cold dark world. As he opened his front door, he whistled the opening bars of Amazing Grace, a tune he had learned at his long departed mother's knee. She had run away with the Evangelist minister who had been brought in to uplift the congregation in the local church when Martin was ten years old. To the best of his knowledge she was making a living, singing, in a Las Vegas nightclub to the present day.

The east wind keened down the street, seeking out every gap and rent in Martin's no longer new overcoat and the slushy snow fell unerringly into the gap between his collar and neck and slithered down his back presenting him with a whole new meaning to the phrase 'sending cold shivers down his spine'

But Martin soldiered bravely on. Fifteen minutes hard struggle in wind and snow brought him to the door of the institute for the destitute which was his chosen destination. As he walked in the door he was greeted by Brother Ignatius.

"Martin, god's blessing on you this harsh morning" he said, but Martin could not help noticing that his normally cheery face bore an ominous troubled look.

"I hate to tell you this Martin, but the coffee machine is broken"

Lady in Red

Sitting in my favourite restaurant and looking out at the frost shrouded trees in St Stephens Green I noticed a beautiful young lady, wearing a flattering red dress, threading through the tables in my direction. as she neared me, I was struck by the way she never looked directly in my direction but seemed to focus on a spot over my right shoulder.

Still blithely ignoring me she walked by, exiting the room, leaving behind a scent of lily of the valley. Turning back to my perfectly cooked rare fillet steak I noticed a folded napkin lying on the floor almost at my toe.

Being, as I am, a confirmed tidier upper I reached down and retrieved the offending piece of paper. As I rolled it up preparatory to disposing of it in the recommended fashion my eye was drawn to some writing on it "Get out NOW, while you still can" screamed the note, written in scarlet lip gloss.

Well, a nod is as good as a wink to a blind horse, to quote the old saying so I hurriedly called for the bill and throwing a bundle of euros on the table I left precipitously. Outside on the steps of the premises I paused to draw a breath of cold, refreshing air. Suddenly a red car drew up to the pavement and the lady in red leaned over and called out the open passenger window "Don't just stand there, get in, we have very little time"

As I, with some trepidation, climbed into the car she slammed it into gear and streamed away from the curb with a squeal of tortured rubber "Were you followed?" she demanded, flicking her eye towards the rear view mirror.

"I'm not accustomed to this type of cloak and dagger carry on" I replied "How would I know if I was followed"

With a hollow laugh she cried "Stick with me and you'll know a lot more than you do now, that's if we survive the next couple of hours"

Recipe for Disaster

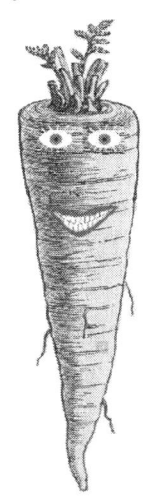

The Mangle Wurzles scrambled frantically through the tangled coils of the internet's unfathomable web of deceit.

They had been tasked by the all glorious high muckamuck Frangrumple the Awkward to find the cure for the plague of Infitesmal Aspirasis of the Prefrontal lobes, which was decimating the ancient and odiferous race of Mangle Wurzles.

As every Youngling of the Mangle Wurzle race Knows, having imbibed it since birth from his, or her, mother's milk, the Internet is an inexhaustible source of all knowledge and misknowledge which only Initiates of the fourth and higher orders may aspire to trawl.

Late in the phase of the third moon, Ginbull, Ningauble, an adept of the upper orders discovered a hitherto forgotten file which had been uploaded back in the Misty dawn of the World Wide Web. The file purported to hold the secret to avoiding the perils of initiating Recipes for Disaster.

"Surely" Thought Ningauble "This is the very thing we need. If ever there was a disaster, then Infitesmal Aspirasis of the Prefrontal Lobes surely is the definitive definition of same.

Now if this file can show how to avoid disasters then the IAPL, for short, is toast"

In a transport of excitement, he rushed to the inner sanctum of Frangrumple the Awkward with the good news. Unfortunately, he disturbed the Awkward one at a rather delicate moment as just then he was immersed in a fuming bath of sulphuric acid, cleansing his carapace in preparation for the Rite of the Enlightenment which took place on the eve of every fourth millennium religiously.

"What do you want" Demanded his exaltedness "Go away and come back at a more opportune moment, can't you see I'm busy?"

"But, but, but" Stammered Ningauble "I'm very sorry your worshipfulness, I think I have the answer to the IAPL plague. I thought you would want to know straight away"

Stuck in a Lift

"What the hell" Jimmy cried as the lift shuddered to a halt between the third and fourth floors. He had been deep in his own thoughts as he and the other passengers were carried to their various floors.

The elderly lady next to him looked upwards towards the roof of the lift and asked, presumably of the God in the Machine, "Hey, I have a doctor's appointment on the sixth floor, I can't be waiting for you to get a move on. So get with the programme willya?"

A scruffy looking teenaged girl spoke up from the back of the lift "Lissen, there's no point in talkin' to the lift, it can't hear ya and if it could it can't talk back. So leave it out, OK?" And to further emphasise her point she blew a large bubble of her gum and allowed it to pop, spreading shards of gum across her face and the lapels of the Tommy Hilfiger suit being worn by a harassed businessman now cowering in the corner.

"I can't stay here" He whimpered, "I'm claustrophobic. If we don't get out immediately, I won't be responsible for what I'll do"

"I mean it" he continued, his voice rising into a shrill falsetto "I can't stand enclosed places"

"Hey dude" said the florist who was carrying a most amazing arrangement of fuchsias, varying in shape, colour and complexity "Look at the flowers man, that'll set your mind at

67

rest, I'd offer you a pull at a spliff, but there's no smoking allowed in this building, The anti smoking Nazis would be on your house five seconds after you lit up"

This was just the sort of thing Jimmy had longed to have happen in his otherwise dreary existence. Assuming an air of omnipotence he said "Now folks, there's no call to get upset. They'll have this sorted in two shakes of a lamb's tail. This sort of thing happens all the time. They have a procedure in place for it I'm sure"

In a quavering voice the elderly Lady piped up with a rousing chorus of Amazing Grace, "Amazing Grace, how sweet the sound that takes a wretch like Me"

"Make the old bat stop" Implored the tall, gaunt man who had been silent until now "The last thing we need right now is caterwauling like that, has anyone got a mobile phone?, maybe we can call the emergency services, they can surely crank this bloody thing up and get us out without too much bother"

Suddenly a voice booed down the lift shaft "Hey, down there. We are working on getting you out of there, but we've hit a small snag. Apparently, the emergency services are on strike and we won't have them here til tomorrow morning. Can we lower some chicken nuggets and chips down to you?"

Austerity

I well remember the good old days. I was born in 1942 in the middle of "The Emergency". Most of the rest of the world had a World War, but we, in Ireland, had "The Emergency"

President Eamonn DeValera, being the wily old git that he was, cobbled up a policy of neutrality which was devised to extract maximum benefit from the protagonists in the conflict, whilst creating minimum annoyance in the process.

Austerity had not been invented in its modern guise way back then, in fact being regarded as austere was something of a compliment in those long ago halcyon days.

However, given the fact that the Germans were torpedoing British shipping, with the avowed intention of starving them into submission, little Ireland was not in a great position to receive supplies from our nearest neighbour, particularly as the neutrality thing was going down like a lead balloon across the pond. Consequently, we were in a state where everything was in short supply, Bread, Butter, Milk, Sugar, Petrol, Coal and pretty much everything you can think of was either sold to the Brits or could not be imported from them. And importing from Germany, even if that were feasible, was frowned upon by the powers that be.

Little wonder then that the anthem being sung on the streets of Dublin was not "A Nation Once Again" but "Starvation

Once Again, No tea, No Sugar, No bread, No butter, Starvation Once Again"

Ration cards were issued to the populace which were designed to ensure that each person received sufficient for their needs, but, not unlike these days, those who were well connected managed to live high off the hog, whilst those at the bottom of the pile went without.

There were no cars on the streets, except for those of people in critical positions, like Doctors and, of course higher Civil Servants and Politicians. The trusty old bicycle was the preferred mode of transport for the greater part of the populace, though even here, spare parts were difficult to find and many of the bikes around town had grass and hay stuffed in the tyres in place of inner tubes, rubber being one of the critical materials required for the prosecution of the war.

Coffee was a luxury almost unknown to the lesser mortals, coming as it did almost exclusively from South America and so being very vulnerable to the marauding U-boats. Tea, on the other hand was procurable as it came from India and Kenya, primarily by land routes until the Continent got in the way. It was prohibitively expensive and heavily rationed.

Central heating was virtually non existent and houses were heated by turf, an inefficient fuel which produced more smoke than heat and was mostly damp to the point of sopping when delivered to the house. Coal was an import which had by the mid forties reached the status of legend, being only available from abroad and subject to the tender ministrations of the aforesaid U-boats.

I could ramble on at great length about the 'Good Old Days' but give me the current austere hard times any day.

Fire Breathing

Billy was a tall, gangly sort of a gink with a distinctive cast in his left eye. He was a committed martial arts aficionado, having reached the seventh dan on his black belt in judo, taekwondo and jiujitsu.

He had arranged to meet his diminutive friend Jim in the Lab, but he hadn't arrived, so Billy had shrugged and silently cursing his friend's tardiness had gone to the dojo on the fourth floor.

Upon opening the door, he had seen an astonishing sight. A tall statuesque lady dressed in extremely revealing, flimsy, trousers and top was inside busily dancing to a mysterious eastern air whilst blowing huge plumes of flame from her nostrils.

Just then Jim entered the room with his breath in his fist "Sorry mate" he said "The mouldy bus was late again, and I hadn't got the right fare, so I had to get off early and walk the last part. What's goin' on anyway. Who's yer wan and what's with the fire breathing crack?"

"I'm not entirely sure" replied Billy "She was here when I got here. Whatever else she's doing it's not martial arts. I'm quite sure of that"

"Should we ask her what's her game?" queried Jim

"Are you out of your freaking mind?" demanded Billy "I would rather face an angry lion than challenge a fire breathing woman. If you're feeling brave, you ask her but if you don't mind, I'll keep well back"

"Well I don't care" boasted Jim "Half naked, fire breathing, woman or not, we booked the dojo, and this is our half hour. She can leave now and practice her andramartins somewhere else. I didn't leave home on a rainy night just to be messed about by some random arsonist. I'm tellin' her to get lost" and he proceeded to do just that.

Sadly, this story might have had a happier ending had he refrained from this extremely rash act.

Walking gingerly up behind the fire breathing lady Jim tapped her on the shoulder and started to say "Lissen missus you can't be carryin' on like that on our time"

Unfortunately, he didn't complete his panegyric. Feeling the tap on her shoulder the fiery lady turned abruptly and gasped in surprise to see the small aggressive man behind her. The effect of her gasp was to expel an enormous blast of fire directly into Jim's face.

"Bloody hell" Billy shouted dashing for the stairs "Someone hit the feckin' fire alarm. The kip is on fire"

An Alien Concept

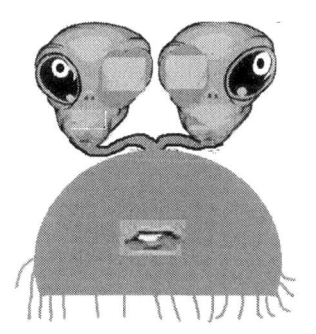

"I didn't feel alone until I met you!" Frankie said to the friendless alien, cowering fearfully under Frank's gooseberry bushes in his overgrown back garden.

"How do you know it was an alien, and a friendless one at that?" I hear you ask.

Well, in the first place it had two heads with an eye in each, a two headed cyclops if you like. It had a strange system of locomotion, with what looked very like millions of tiny hairs poking out all around the circumference of its body which was shaped like an upturned porridge bowl. These hair like appendages thrashed about almost like the oars on an old style roman galley, enabling the creature to inch along at a painfully slow pace.

If that wasn't enough to convince Frankie that he was face to face with an honest to god alien, the large, slobbering mouth somewhere in the region of its chest was enough to put the tin lid on the idea.

Given the unlikely appearance of his nocturnal visitor, it's slow motion gait and the fact that there was no sign of a companion alien, it may not be surprising that Frankie that it was a unique specimen, at least in this neck of the woods.

"Take me to your leader" Frankie said, in a portentous voice. For some reason, perhaps a youth spent watching bad sci fI movies, he had convinced himself that this was the appropriate manner in which one addressed an extraterrestrial.

Not too surprisingly the creature's response sounded rather more like the croaking of an adenoidal bullfrog and Frankie could not make any sense out of its utterances.

Suddenly before his horrified eyes, Frankie's pet pit bulldog ran, barking madly out of the house and bounded towards the, obviously unwanted visitor.

"Heel Bertram. Bad dog, sit, sit immediately" Frankie was just a couple of seconds too late with his doggy admonition. The visitor from elsewhere opened its mouth impossibly wide, swelled up to about three times its original size and with an audible slurp, extended a yard long, leprous green tongue and snatched the unfortunate Bertram and, to bowdlerise the music hall song "he swallered our Bertram 'ole"

All of the foregoing might have been forgivable, except that Frankie was inordinately fond of the unwise canine.

"Bad alien" He cried, stamping his foot, "Give me my dog back, that sort of behaviour is way out of line in this neighbourhood. In extreme circumstances we have been known to take out injunctions forcing dog owners to maintain order and control over their pets but, after all, Bertram was only looking out for my safety and marking his territory into the bargain"

With an enigmatic blink of its cyclonic eyes, the alien rose, buzzing into the air and flew straight up and out of sight.

The Book Chair

If I had had a library the book chair would have had a place of honour in it. But since I don't, the book chair lived in the living room in front of the television, far from the kitchen and it's culinary temptations.

Last week as I sat at ease reading a spooky story by John Connolly, I was startled out of my wits by a deep voice seemingly out of thin air and directly behind my head.

"Harry" the voice queried "Why are you reading that scary story? It's not your usual type of read"

Now you may wonder why this voice startled me so much. The reason was that in my own mind I had the house entirely to myself. My immediate superior had taken herself off on one of her visits to her sisters in the wilds of Co Meath and by the grace of God there were none of the ever expanding tribe of grandchildren thrashing around underfoot.

Consequently, the intrusion of this voice was both unusual and unexpected. Adding to my confusion and unease was that I did not recognise it.

Turning my head, I was even more surprised to find nobody in the room with me.

"Who just spoke?" I demanded.

"I did" The voice replied, again apparently out of thin air.

"Who are you?" I demanded "Come out of wherever you are hiding yourself so I can get a look at you"

75

"I'm right here in front of you, you gobshite, open your eyes will you"

"What do you mean, here in front of me. There's nothing here but me and the chair"

"Well duh" said the voice "If there's nothing but you and the chair and you aren't talking to yourself, who does that leave?"

"You don't mean, Are you telling me, Is that voice coming from my book chair? how could that be?"

"It's quite simple really" the chair replied "I've been reading an awful lot of tripe over your shoulder for the past sixty years and to tell the truth I'm just about up to here with it. I've decided to make my presence known and give you some input into your reading selections going forward.

Furthermore, I've also decided that if what you've been reading is any indication of the general standard of the stuff that's out there I could easily do better myself. So, I've decided that I'm going to dictate a magnum opus and you're going to type it, then we're going to publish it and it'll be an instant best seller. We'll make a fortune out of it"

"We'll call it 'Readings From the Chair' I'll be interviewed on television and radio and get to meet Pat Kenny and stuff. It'll be great craic"

The chair is gone now, burnt to cinders and replaced by a Swedish thing from IKEA.

Perilous Habit

It was the first time I killed a man, but, in fairness he badly needed killing. He had the most annoying habit of prefacing whatever he wanted to say with the phrase 'do yeh know whar I'm goin to tell yeh".

Now the first time you hear a phrase like that it probably causes a smile and the second time it may be found to be mildly repetitive but after hearing it every day, five days a week in the staff canteen at lunch it begins to wear on the nerves.

Finally, I could stand it no longer and I started to plan a drastic solution to the problem. At first, I had no homicidal intentions but the more I thought about it the clearer it seemed to me that only extreme measure would meet the case.

Say, for instance, I decided to merely incapacitate the bloody nuisance and put him out of action for a while, then inevitably he'd be back again as obtuse as ever with even more reasons to demand 'Do you know what I'm going to tell yeh?

No, on mature reflection the only sure way to resolve the issue was to have him pop his clogs and the sooner the better.

Things like this need to be carefully thought out, going into the canteen and slicing him up with a carving knife might be highly satisfactory but both the employer and the fuzz tend to look askance at that sort of carry on. Subtlety is the watchword here. Poisoning might be good but poor old Annie the canteen cook might be blamed for his untimely demise and

God knows her cooking is pretty awful but even she doesn't deserve the stigma of having one of her best customers allegedly dying from her pathetic attempts at the Wednesday shepherd's pie.

An industrial accident looks like a perfect proposition but even given his extreme clumsiness and long history of workplace incidents killing someone in an industrial accident isn't as easy as it looks.

I did persuade him to come for a walk down the canal one day and contrived to trip him and cause him to take a cannonball into the murky water but unfortunately I had neglected to check beforehand and it turned out that he was a junior swimming champion in his youth, so he survived.

The following day he walked into the canteen and in a loud voice said "Do yiz know whar I'm goin' ta tell yiz?"

Losing all sense of restraint, I rose up and strangled him to the tumultuous applause of the other diners.

The judge called it justifiable homicide.

Flying Anteater

That Michael O'Leary, I'm going to report him to the Society for The Racial Perpetuation Of The Endangered Species Of The Lesser Spotted Giant Aardvark. What sort of an airline does he run, anyway? He doesn't provide room for a twenty five Stone, perfectly behaved insect Hoover upper. I bet if he wanted to bring one of his bloody racehorses to France, he'd soon find room for it on his mouldy aeroplane.

I mean, it's not like they are any great shakes, those planes. They have wings alright, and engines and stuff but so too do all the other aeroplanes going about the skies, so what's so great about his planes?

Speaking for myself, and some other members of the aforesaid Society For The racial Perpetuation Of The Endangered Species Of The Lesser Spotted Giant Aardvark, I can't recall ever hearing about one of our beloved, furry and extremely useful, long nosed friends being refused passage on any mode of transport, plane, ship, bus or donkey cart. This ruling by an infamous despot is just insufferable.

It's not in my nature to wish harm to others, just ask my brother if you don't believe me, but really, if a plague of African fire ants were to materialise in the same Michael O'Leary's trousers and proceed to make life most uncomfortable for him, I would hesitate to ask Aristotle, for that's my friendly Aardvark's name to intervene on his behalf.

Aristotle himself if left to his own devices would, I am sure, be more than happy to intervene on the rascally chief executives' behalf. He is, after all, inordinately fond of an

African fire ant snack whenever the opportunity presents itself but in my humble opinion to seek to relieve his distress would be above and beyond the call of duty, as far as Aristotle is concerned.

So far as I am concerned, any flights which myself and Aristotle plan in future will involve the consumption of copious draughts of Red Bull, it gives you wings, so they tell me.

Eighteenth Birthday

"You're only telling me this now? What sort of monsters are you anyway? The only upside to this story is that you're not my real parents, I'm quite sure that no natural parent would keep a thing like that secret, and on my first day of college too"

"Well, there's more..."

"More? How could there be more? Am I not cursed enough without anything else?"

"It seems that your Father was talking last night in the Happy Knacker and you know how he gets garrulous when he has a few in? Well he let the cat out of the bag"

"Let the cat out of the bag? Don't tell me, he didn't, oh sweet Jaysus, he told that snot nosed bitch, Freda Moloney's father that I'm not human, didn't he? That's takes the bleeding biscuit. You can be sure of one thing, I'm not going next nor near that college after this fiasco, no bleeding way!"

"While we are in this new open forum, let's tell everybody everything frame of mind, are there any other little tiny details I should know about myself? Like who are my real parents? Possibly the master and mistress of the universe maybe, or more likely some intergalactic criminals who've been locked up on some frozen asteroid between Mars and Jupiter for wiping out whole civilisations. Probably serving multiple life sentences in a cryogenic suspension pod"

"Actually, there is one small thing. You know the wardrobe in your room downstairs? Well it has a false panel in the back, if you twist the fifth hanger from the left hand side counter clockwise fourteen times it'll open the panel and you'll see a flight of stairs heading downwards. When the door opens, the lights will go on, so it's not spooky or anything. Mind you, we've never gone down ourselves, we don't go in for the risky, daredevil stuff like going down mysterious stairs into unknown depths. Given your stated objection to going to college you might like to give it a shot."

"That really makes up for the past eighteen years of lies and deception, so it does. I apparently have a choice of going to college, where I'll be the butt of all the sneers and jokes of the freshers or I can take a trip down a dark stairs leading to god knows where? All things considered I think I'll head off into the Sahara desert and see if I can't find myself an Arab Sheik who'll throw me over his saddle and take me away to a life of unimaginable luxury in his oil rich kingdom somewhere over there"

"Listen, here's an email address, I don't know who it goes to, but when we got you, they told us that if this conversation ever came up we should give it to you, and you could use it if you liked??"

The Fourth Wall

"But mammy, I'm not telling lies, I can see the fourth wall" Little Max was obviously distressed.

"Max" his already strung out mother, she was trying, mainly in vain, to juggle the raising of three boisterous children under the age of seven, plus hold down a high powered job in public relations and deal with a ne'er do well husband whose sole contribution to domestic harmony was to roll in regularly, drunk as a skunk, said "Creativity is all very well and good. But as we all know, very well, there is no such thing as a fourth wall. In the entire history of the world the absolute maximum number of possible walls is fixed in stone, pardon the pun, at three. Two is all right, one is acceptable but four is anathema. So no more, OK?

"I absolutely know that I can see the fourth wall" Three year old Max muttered under his breath as he snatched the last crust of bread off his older brother's plate and ran out the door.

"Ma" the older boy wailed "That little bollix just swiped the last bit off my plate, I was saving that. The last bite is always the best and now he's gone and ruined it"

"One for sorrow, two for joy" Murmured the mother as she prepared the magpies for the dinner, "Three for a girl and four for a boy" she continued absentmindedly, dropping the partly plucked, tiny corpses of the birds into the stew pot.

Suddenly she jumped as Max's sister, the oddly named Peterkin, started to wail loudly.

"Oh no, mother" she wept "How could you, you've brought bad luck down on us all. If Max can't see the fourth wall, how can we eat a fourth bird? It just doesn't make any sense. If four of one thing is bad, then four of another can't be good. Sauce for the goose, after all"

Into the midst of the hullabaloo Max returned bearing an enormous platter with all manner of wonderful foods piled high. "Now" He demanded "Will you believe me now? Anyone who subscribes to that fourth wall being bad luck can suck on the scabby magpies' bones. As for me, anything I want, I can get. I can see the fourth wall, don't you know?

Making Tracks

As Sammy stood between the railway tracks which seemed to extend into infinity he was struck by an errant thought. "Now that I've made the decision and it's too late to turn back, I'm scared out of my wits. I should never have gotten into this ridiculous situation in the first place. What could I have been thinking about?"

Actually, Sammy knew very well what he had been thinking about. She was a stunning beauty, the absolute epitome of Sammy's dream girl. Such a pity that he hadn't let his brain into gear before his libido drove him to acquiesce to her suggestion that they should travel the tracks together on boxcars and let the night fall on them wherever they might find themselves. The proper term, he believed was hobo.

All seemed to be going swimmingly until the time came for them to catch their first boxcar. To Sammy's limited experience the trains seemed to be travelling at frightening speed. This did not daunt the light of his life, however.

"C'mon" she called, racing after the accelerating train and reaching up to grasp the bar on the door. She swung her lithe body up and onto the floor of the empty car and reached her hand out to Sammy

"Move yer arse" She shouted over the noise of the panting Diesel engine "It's not going to wait for you, you know. Just grab hold of my hand and I'll give you boost up. You'll catch on easily"

Sammy, who had not run anywhere since his childhood, puffed as he lumbered after the train which seemed to him to be picking up speed faster than his ability to keep up, was unable to answer due to the shortness of breath and chest pains which seemed set fair to be the end of him.

Panting and gasping he stretched out his hand and in what he realised was a metaphor for his entire life he felt the touch of her fingertips for a brief instant before the train took her out of his reach.

"Too bad Sammy" She called back to him as he collapsed prostrate on the cold sleepers "Maybe we'll meet sometime when our tracks cross in the future"

Sammy thought he never heard a lonelier sound than the hum of the tracks as the girl of his dreams retreated into the gathering dusk.

Technicolour Cake.

Joe, in fairness to him, was the most equable person you could meet in a long day's walk. He was famous in his own circle of friends and relatives as a man who is kind, thoughtful and considerate, a judge of good whiskey and women, and a friend to dumb animals.

Unfortunately, he does have one character quirk, not to describe it as a fault. He is, among his other accomplishments, a fully fledged and paid up member of the Society of Gourmets, Ireland Chapter. This is an honour conferred on very few people. However, here's where the quirk comes in. Joe tends to let his enthusiasms run away with him on occasion.

The culinary standards which he practices are of the highest and he inclines towards demanding similar qualities in his friends. Consequently, those whose cooking is not, in his estimation, up to scratch, always have the invitations to dine which are sent to him, declined, courteously, but firmly. Those who do meet his exacting requirements are, in turn, likely to leave him off the guest list owing to the cussedness of his character regarding the culinary arts.

In consequence of the aforesaid, poor Joe rarely dined in company and so he was forced to rely on his own company at table.

The inevitable consequence of this isolation came to a head one cold November day when Joe's letterbox rattled and the postman, one of his friends, called out that he had a letter. Joe, as intimated earlier received very few letters as his bills were invariably settled on the Internet and his invoices arrived in the same manner.

He was, in fact quite excited to receive this missive and rushed to the hall door to find out who his correspondent might be. Imagine his astonishment when he found that his Grandnephew, Robert, was inviting him to a birthday party. He was not exactly fond of young children and he hardly knew this urchin, but he now felt so isolated, dining wise, that he determined to accept the child's no doubt well meant invitation.

He suffered through the kid's games, the atrociously bad clown/magician until the food arrived. Confronted by an array of fish fingers, chicken tenders, mini hamburgers and copious quantities of orange squash his endurance snapped, and he lost his cool to an extraordinary extent.

Grabbing the, to him, hideous technicolour birthday cake he upended it over poor Roberts head and stormed out vowing never to have anything to do with this class of abomination in the future.

Personally, I thought that Joe was the last person on earth I'd expect to do something like that, but needs must when the devil drives, to use a saying which my sainted mother was very fond of.

Stone cushion

"Me ass is fractured" said Sylvester swan as he thrust himself up into the wide blue yonder. "I've been sitting, overlong, on that stone cushion"

"Some might think that Stone Cushion is an oxymoron" said his lifelong mate Fionnuala. In this enlightened state gays are not the only ones who are not allowed to marry and although Sylvia and Sylvester had enjoyed connubial bliss for twenty years, they remained only mates. This was not a big issue for them, however, as they were sublimely unaware of the benefits, real or imagined, of the married state.

Fionnuala was actually one of the original Children of Lir and was condemned to live forever as a swan. Sylvester, who had met Fionnuala as a young cygnet and was immediately smitten with her beauty and enchanting air of mystery had proposed mate hood as soon as he was of age.

Fionnuala, sick and tired of the company of her three brothers, held captive by the same spell as herself, and feeling a little randy had accepted Sylvester's proposal and somewhere in the courting and canoodling had forgotten to reveal her interesting condition to him. He was therefore in blissful ignorance not only that his mate was a couple of hundred years older than him but, all going well was likely to outlive him by another six hundred more. Still, she was a fine looking bird and always ready for a little bit of how's your father? so he didn't enquire too deeply into her family circumstances or previous history.

Seeing Sylvester flying in carefree circles overhead she commenced her launch sequence along the river where they had made their home, calling out as she rose in the air "Hold on Syl, I fancy a bit of a wing stretch myself. Why don't we go visit my brother Conn down in Lough Derg, it's been a long time since we were down there. I heard on the grapevine that Fiachra may be visiting also"

"Sounds good to me" he replied "It's always good craic to visit your brothers though Fiachra seems a little dour about someone called Aoife. He seems to think she caused him some injury in past times, I couldn't quite make it out the last time I was talking to him, but he was a little bit out of it, maybe because he'd been grazing on magic mushrooms or something. He was muttering about spells and stuff. Maybe he needs a mate too, what do you think?"

Best Laid Plans

      Struggling to his knees Jimmy pulled the engagement ring from his pocket. It had taken him months of arduous searching to find exactly the right one. It featured a huge, square amethyst flanked by groups of diamonds on both sides and had cost him the equivalent of the ransom which might be demanded for the king of a small Kingdom.

      "Darling Felicity, will you be my bride" he pleaded, to the tremendous enjoyment of the other tourists gathered, teeth chattering, on the highest balcony of the Eiffel Tower in Paris on a particularly cold February day.

      "Get up you old fool" snapped Felicity "You're embarrassing yourself, and worse still me too"

      Totally stupefied Jimmy sought to catch his breath. This was not the response he had anticipated. He had carefully selected the ring because the Amethyst was the February birthstone and Felicity's birthday fell on Valentine's Day. He had booked a holiday which the brochure had described as 'Four, fabulous days and nights in the most romantic city in the world, including a trip to the top of the Eiffel Tower'

      "Jesus, that's harsh" he said, tears in his eyes, whether from an excess of emotion or from the biting wind which was screaming about them on the exposed balcony. "That's just about the meanest thing anyone has ever said to me"

"What were you thinking of?" Demanded Felicity "You're seventy five years old. Marriage at your age would be the finish of you! Besides, what made you think I wanted to get married anyway?"

"But, but, but" stammered Jimmy "We've been courting for twenty years now. I thought it was time to bring our relationship to the next level. You've never given me any reason to think that you weren't interested. All the magazines say that women want to be married"

"I'm not that fond of wedding cake" snarled Felicity as Jimmy painfully clambered to his feet. "I've been married three times before and believe me, it doesn't get any better with repetition. So put that Pound Shop thing away and let's get off this bloody hurricane perch. I don't know which is worse, your idiotic behaviour or this blasted wind but I'm outta here right now"

Spelling Bee

Patrick was becoming somewhat apprehensive as he made his way up the long, deeply potholed drive towards Ghastly Manor. He had been invited to join in The Fifth International Spelling Bee Competition in an email from someone he'd never heard of before. Under normal circumstances Patrick did not respond to unsolicited invitations from unknown sources and certainly not when they arrived by email. But in this case the eyewateringly large amount of prize money had proved too tempting to turn down.

Right now, though, as the evening light began to fail and the soaring leafless beech trees lining the avenue started to look uncannily like banshees waving in the wind which had just begun to pick up, his determined avarice was getting less compelling the further he walked.

As he had almost convinced himself to turn back and forego his chance at all that filthy lucre the avenue bent to the right and the trees fell away on both sides.

"Holy God" whispered Patrick as he gazed in awe at the huge Georgian pile now revealed. The light was now almost gone, and the clouds had assumed a weird purple hue yet there were no lights to be seen in the house.

With sinking heart, he continued towards the house and mounting the broad, broken steps he pulled the bell pull. Immediately a loud clangour of off key bells broke out inside, accompanied by the frantic barking of an obviously very large dog.

As Patrick contemplated making a run for it the massive door creaked open on rusty hinges, revealing a dusty vestibule filled to capacity with a bewildering array of distressed furniture of all vintages and ages. As he stood there nervously looking about a feeble voice spoke "Well don't just stand there with the door swinging open, you'll let all the heat out. Shut it son, shut it"

At first glance Patrick could not see the speaker but on further inspection he saw an old, very old lady dressed in clothes more suited to a lady of the eighteenth century, sitting huddled in a high backed wing chair. The chair was drawn up to a tiny flickering group of wet sods of turf in an enormous fireplace.

"Come in, son" The old crone said "Come closer dearie, my old eyes are not what they used to be. Come closer to the fire so I can get a good look at you"

"I think I'm in the wrong house" Said Patrick "I was invited to a spelling Bee in Ghastly Manor. Is this Ghastly Manor?"

"No, no" Wheezed the crone "No mistake, this is indeed Ghastly Manor, but I have to tell you that the spelling bee thing was just a ruse to get you here. I have different plans for you this evening"

As she spoke the front door slammed shut with a thunderous bang and Patrick found that it was impossible to open it again.

Turning to the crone he demanded "What's going on here? I came here in good faith to participate in a spelling bee, please unlock this door immediately or I'll be forced to take measures" He wasn't entirely sure what he meant by 'taking measures', but it sounded sufficiently menacing to him. After all she was only an old hag and he was a young man, he was bound to come out in front in anything which might develop, wasn't he?

Hearing a scrabbling noise behind him he saw the biggest wolfhound he could ever have imagined stalking across the broken tiles towards him....

Peasouper

Season of mists me arse, I can't see a damn thing in this cursed peasouper. How in the name Of all that's good and holy am I supposed to make my way home in this? If I was to be responsible and careful, I'd ditch the car and walk, but it must be four miles, for God's sake! My dickey ticker would pack up before I made it a quarter of that, bugger it, I'll stick to the old jam jar.

Jeez, it's getting worse, I can't see beyond the bonnet. I really should give up on the driving, it's just not safe enough. What was that? I felt a bump just then; I must have hit something.

What to do? I expect it might have been a dog or a cat, the world would be a better place if there were fewer domestic animals allowed in the cities, so one less is a bonus. But hold on, what if it was a person, it might have been a policeman out to clean up the streets of the crowd of scroungers who infest the inner city, maybe I should stop and check.

On the other hand, this is not a very salubrious part of town, it might have been someone who banged the car just to get me to stop so that they could hijack me, God knows I would make a poor mark for a hijack, the car is a fourteen year old Toyota and I have exactly three euros and fifteen cents on my person. But these bozos don't know that, they can't see beyond their noses so it could be a Maserati for all they know. With its busted silencer it certainly sounds like a Maserati.

To hell with it, I'll just keep on keeping on, I'll check the papers tomorrow and see if there are any reports of someone being knocked down. Mind you, I don't know for sure exactly where I am at the moment, so I won't know in the morning if it was me or someone else who knocked down the pedestrian, if any pedestrian was knocked down at all.

Look at that, it's a beautiful morning, the sun is shining and all's well with the world, I was really out of it last night, that fog had me bewildered. I'm glad I didn't report an accident that might never have happened. The fuzz would have locked me up and thrown away the key, acting on the basis that if I was confessing, then I must be guilty of something or other.

Oh dear, the news headline says Hit and Run Killer sought! What to do, what to do.

Plane Companions

"Oh, hello, it must be twenty years since I saw you" To be absolutely honest, if I never saw her again it would be too soon. She was a colossal snob then and from the looks of her Gucci boots, Givenchy dress and the waft of Chanel number five she hadn't changed much.

"Em, do I know you?" She queried

Damn and blast, there she goes again, she always had a unique way of making me feel small. "Yes, Josephine, you do know me, very well. We sat side by side for seven years all through our primary school years"

"I beg your pardon, it's Peter Mason, isn't it. You've changed, I wouldn't have known you. What are you doing with yourself these days?"

"I'm working as a thoracic surgeon and I have a teaching position in the College of Surgeons" I replied in my snippiest tone of voice.

"Ah, yes, you were always best in class at video games. I see in the Irish Times that surgeons who were good at those type of games are likely to be less prone to making mistakes. Personally, I don't place much faith in conventional medicine. I have a little old lady who lives in my gatehouse and she has the cure for most, if not all, of the maladies which afflict the human body" This was delivered in tones of the utmost condescension.

"Little old ladies with cures are all well and good, but in my experience, and I have a lot of experience, when real hardship strikes their nostrums tend to go by the wayside. You know the old saying 'there are no atheists in the trenches' It's not beyond the bounds of possibility that you might find yourself needing the skills of someone in my line of work" My own delivery had developed a crust of ice on it as the conversation progressed.

"Actually" I continued "I'm pretty sure that I did some work on your Dad about a year ago, how's he doing, by the way?"

"He died shortly after the operation" The conversational temperature dropped to a new, frigid level.

"Oh well, win some, lose some" I philosophised as I called the flight attendant and asked if I could change my seat.

Every dog has his day.

"If ever there was a load of old bollix, that takes the biscuit" Snarled Bernard the Bulldog "I've been a dog all my life and not only have I not had my own day, but I never came across any other dog who had had his, or her, day either"

"Now if we were to take the other saying 'It's a dog's life' it would make more sense. I mean if you want to figure out what a day in the life is like for a member of the canine fraternity, all you have to do is listen to the songs on the radio.

First off there's the old favourite 'How much is that doggy in the window' I mean how demeaning is it to be displayed in a shop window for every little snot nosed kid to be drooling over you, maybe to take you home, or not if the price was not agreeable to her miserable, penny pinching parents. Or worse still what about the other doggies in the windows, the ones without the waggly tails, who's going to look out for them?"

"Then there's 'Old Shep'' There he was, minding his own business when he hears the screams of the kid in the old swimming hole. Does he do what any right minded dog would do and roll over a go back to sleep, does he what. No he jumps in and helps drag to stupid little bread snapper out. And what does he get for his trouble? He gets a worn out, meatless bone thrown to him and a bed, as usual, in the barn"

"All things considered the whole concept of every dog having his day is seriously flawed. How would you legislate for such a thing, I mean, who would you put in charge of seeing that each and every mutt got his day? The ISPCA has enough trouble looking out for distressed donkeys and abandoned racehorses without trying to police the 'Every Dog Day Rule'.

We might apply To the European Union for equal status for dogs, but five Minutes after we got it, the bleeding cats would be squalling and wailing for the same, and following close behind would be the ferrets, the rats, the voles, what is a vole anyway, and then the lesser animals like the horses and cows. It would be a legislative nightmare, I tell you"

"Given the foregoing, I personally intend to adopt the attitude of the dog in the country and western song:

> "The hound dog's howlin' he's so forlorn,
> he's howlin' cause he's sittin" on a thorn,
> The laziest dog as ever was born,
> He's jest too tired to move over"

Alice and the Cheshire Cat

"What road should I take" Demanded Alice.

"Where do you want to go?" queried the Cheshire Cat

"I don't know" replied Alice in a cantankerous voice.

"Then it doesn't matter. If you don't know where you are going, any road will get you there" The Cat was in full put down mode.

"Are you always such a pain in the arse, or did someone take the milk out of your tea this morning?   If I wanted snot nosed commentary I would have gone to the Red Queen, though mostly she only says, 'off with his head' She seems to have a bit of a hang up with the head offing thing. Anyway, you might as well do your disappearing into nothingness trick. For all the good you add to the conversation you might as well vanish up your own arse as hang around here. I'll ask elsewhere for advice"

"That's easy for you to say, we've been stuck in this lift for the past three hours and from what I can gather we'll be here for considerably longer. We should try to keep the conversation on a civil footing if possible, there's just the two of us, after all"

"Three hours you say, how time flies when you're having fun" Said Alice now into full flights of sarcasm "What made you so wise and your mother so foolish? Have you got some form of internal communication system or something, I didn't hear anyone tell you how long it's going to be before they let us out of this blasted immobile, mobile prison"

"As it happens, I operate on a couple of different planes, so one of my personas is here in your delightful company and another is in the basement with the engineer from Otis, the elevator people. In between whinging about what an up and down business the elevator trade is, he's told me that he's waiting for parts for the gizmo that makes the yoke go up and down. Apparently, there's a massive protest in town and traffic is hung up for forty miles around. It'll take hours to clear the jam. I can tell you this because my two personas are connected by means of cosmic strings and anything which I know, he knows, and anything which he knows, I know, if you get my meaning"

"Cosmic strings! I never heard such bullshit, you are a cat, just a cat, nothing more and nothing less. I've seen the fading away thing but that's as much as I believe you can do. This string theory of yours is utter bunkum"

"Bunkum is it, well here we go, I'm going to fade away and take my leave of you, I don't need to put up with your lip any longer. Me and my various personas will go look for more congenial company elsewhere" and he faded away, starting at his tail and proceeding forwards until all that remained of him was his toothy grin. In due course, that also faded to nothingness.

"I wish I had some of his cosmic string" Thought Alice "I'd weave it into a rope and climb down this blasted lift shaft"

Lethal Mix

Take two parts Paddy,
Six parts Jenny,
A dash of Father John
Add liberal quantities of alcoholic beverage
Mix thoroughly and allow to macerate for a couple of hours

"Listen" slurred Paddy, who had drunk, not wisely, but too well. "The thing with our Jenny, saving your presence Father John, is that she talks a bit over much, know what I mean?"

Jenny, never the most delicate of flowers, even when stone cold sober, which on this occasion she most certainly was not snarled "Just because you haven't got the wit to tie two words together unless you're pissed out of your mind doesn't give you leave to be bad mouthing other, more verbose people. And leave poor Father John out of this, there's no call to be hiding behind the clergy's cassocks. If you have something to say, come right out and say it"

"Now, now" Intoned Father John in his best Sunday morning sermonising tone of voice "I'm quite sure that there's no bad feeling meant in either of your comments. We should all take care to allow space for all members of God's children to express themselves"

"Tha's easy for you to shay" Spluttered Paddy "You don't hafta Lissen to her goin on, day and night until you don't know if yer on yer arse or yer elbow. It's a pure disaster, so it is"

With face as red as her flaming curls Jenny heaped scorn on both Paddy and Father John "Men" she snarled "You don't know the half of it. There's Paddy in his cushy job in the civil service, nothing to do all day but sup cups of coffee and ignore the phones incessant ringing. And as for the good Father there, he spends his time going round to all the old biddys in the parish taking little drops of a heart warmer in each house so that by day's end he's only fit to sit with his feet up watching television.

Now me, on the other hand, I'm at home here with a small baby all day and as soon as I get her settled and asleep, her brothers and sister come in from school and wake her up with their shouting and arguing. Then Paddy comes home, upsets the kids, has his dinner handed to him and then goes out to the pub with his mates. No wonder I'm starved for some adult conversation"

"The curse of the seven snotty orphans on the both of you" Said Father John "Think of all the poor and downtrodden in the world who would be happy to be in either of your positions. Now sort yourselves out. I'm off to the pub, see you Sunday at mass, as usual"

True Love's Diamond

"Awaken my inner diamond how are you" Harry cried "Easy for some, here I am stuck in front of this empty frame trying my best to write the 'Great Twenty First Century Irish Novel' and all I get for prompts is inner diamonds and blank frames. It's just not good enough. I'm joining a different writers group next week, or maybe the week after so I am" and turning on his heel he stormed out of the room.

"Thank god for that" said Arnold, "I thought he'd never go, I'm just about sick of his constant whinging about The Great Twenty First Century Novel, anyone would think he was some sort of a writer or something. Has anyone seen anything he's written, No? Well good riddance to him I say"

"Ah now, you can't be like that, after all this writing lark isn't easy, is it. There's always a good excuse not to write and the prompts lately have been either very obscure or just plain boring, now haven't they?" Carmel could always be relied on to pour oil on troubled waters. Little did she know that in this case she had, herself, whipped up a storm of biblical proportions.

"What do you mean" Demanded Jimmy "I'll have you know that I spent hours and gallons of ink making out the blank frames prompt. If anyone has any better ideas, I think they should bring them forward, it'll be a cold day in hell before I bring another prompt to this bloody bunch of ingrates. Sharper than a feckin serpents tooth, how are ye"

"Who is in charge of this gig anyway" queried Fred "The whole problem as far as I'm concerned is that there's no one person in charge. This is what happens when everyone is allowed to wander off on their own bat. There's no structure. Without structure we won't get anywhere. I think we need an executive committee with various subcommittees for finance, entertainment, discipline etc. I would volunteer to be chair of the discipline committee if there was one, myself"

"On a point of order, I'd like to propose an item for the agenda" Brendan said in a loud voice "I would like to put forward a motion proposing 'The Split'"

Rose of Tralee

Dear sir or madam,

I have no wish or desire to be included in the group of would be escorts for your Rose of Tralee thing. No sirree bob, I wouldn't touch that gig with a ten foot pole, I want to be a contestant in the actual Rose of Tralee contest itself. Now I'm well aware that you've never had a male rose before, but as it now appears that the gates of this particular contest seem to be open to all, I see no good reason why I should be excluded merely on the grounds of my gender.

Before we go any further, I must point out that denying me this opportunity would, in my opinion, be a gross infringement on my inalienable rights under our constitution, God bless it. Not that I would wish to imply that, should I fail to be considered for this prestigious title, that I will immediately slap you guys with a writ of injunction and sue you for all your worldly goods, yea, even unto the third and fourth generation.

I would not want you to get the wrong end of the stick here, my brother in law is a prominent barrister and I've gone to the bother of getting his respected opinion, legal and moral, and he assures me that if push comes to shove, we would win such a case, hands down. No bother.

So, in the interests of a peaceful outcome to my request, I recommend that you shoot me out the application documents and a stamped addressed envelope for my completed paperwork without delay.

I can understand that this might cause somewhat of a rustle in the dovecote as the girls may find it undesirable to share their changing rooms and sleeping arrangements with a mere male, but I assure you that I am certifiably harmless, having had the snip done some three years ago.

    Furthermore, if all other courses fail, I will accept that I should dress and sleep in solitary splendour should that be the only course open to me.

    Yours Hopefully,

    Jeremiah Doherty

    Dear Mr Doherty,

    Many thanks for your kind and thoughtful letter. Unfortunately owing to a flood of applications for entries to the competition, many of them, in fact well over seventy percent of them, from men, we find ourselves fully subscribed with male contestants, there are however several vacancies on our escort panel, and we would be more the happy to include you in that group.

    Declan O'Rourke,

    Honorary Secretary,

    Rose of Tralee Festival,

    Selection Committee.

Job Offer

The ad had caught her eye on her way into work 'Would you like a more challenging job? Tired of the daily mundanity of the normal office grind? Go to www.enticingthings.it for an introductory offer you can't refuse'

"That sounds like it might be just up my street" she thought "I'm just about fed up to the back teeth with this gig in the Department and the supervisor with the chronic halitosis. I should just check out the website on my iPhone" and reaching into her capacious handbag she rooted round looking for Jimmy.

Well maybe everyone doesn't name their iPhones but in this case, Maria had a thing about naming her personal items. She paused with the phone in her hand and thought

"Am I mad or what, I work for the Government, there's no need for me to be wasting either my call minutes, nor my battery. I have nothing to do in the dire dungeon and all day to do it, so I'll wait till I get in and get myself a cup of coffee, then I'll check out the website"

Later in the morning, it had been a somewhat hectic one, unusual for the normal quiet of the grave imposed by the Halitosis man, but Jenny had arrived unexpectedly with news that the pair in HR had actually eloped together after fifteen years of surreptitious philandering.

It seems that his wife had sussed him out and had had him followed, finding that he was doing the rude thing with yer wan, she set yer wan's husband on them. The husband took it a bit badly and in the ensuing altercation lover boy sustained a broken pelvis, which, if nothing else, put a bit of a crimp in their illicit love life. Yer wan then uttered an ultimatum to him:

"no more philandering, we get hitched or the jig is up" Apparently, he found himself in sore need of nursing care, so he agreed.

Anyway, as Maria finally got set up at her desk, she remembered the website

"Oh bugger" she moaned "What was the name? I thought at the time that it was a cool sort of name, but now I can't remember it"

She spent the remainder of the day trying out various names and combinations of names, but nothing worked.

"Hell" she cried, "I'll just have to check it out on the bus in the morning and start all over again"

Valkyrie

The last time I saw her she was heading off into the sunset, riding on a winged horse and wearing a silver, one piece, skin tight suit and an enormous gloriously plumed helmet made of white gold.

This struck me as a bit strange as she was, up until then, employed as a server in the canteen of the huge foundry where I was the head chef. There was, to the best of my knowledge, nothing about her to suggest that she had super human powers or that she was likely to become a participant in the Ride of the Valkyries. She was, to all intents and purposes a normal, rather easy going type with a husband and two and a half kids at home.

Her transformation came about, as far as can be ascertained, when the dreaded axe was wielded by the catering manager and she found herself downsized as a result of the decline in the market for items cast by the foundry. There is not a big call for brass candlesticks anymore. This should not have come as a surprise to her or indeed to anyone as the numbers of diners in the canteen had been steadily falling over the course of the years of devastation since the economic collapse.

Nevertheless Valerie, for that was her name, took the whole thing as a deeply personal affront. Heading home to break the bad news to her husband, Eric, a shiftless and idle man whose primary ambition consisted in being within easy reach of the fridge door and not too far from the couch and the television remote, Val was involved in an accident with a double forty foot container truck and trailer combination.

For most people travelling on foot such an incident would prove fatal. But not Val.

The truck smashed into her as she crossed the road, entirely legally on a pedestrian crossing, but instead of instant obliteration for Val the truck received a lady shaped dent in its bonnet, the engine block sundered, sending out huge clouds of steam and oily smoke. The driver was ejected through the windscreen, he had neglected to clunk click as has been advised by road safety experts internationally.

Fortunately for him he landed in Valerie's waiting arms. Placing him gently on the pavement she admonished him "You need to be more careful sir; you never know what's around the corner. Just this morning I was unexpectedly fired from my job, otherwise I wouldn't have been on this crossing just now and this accident would never have happened" she was not at all put out by the fact that she should, by all rights, have been squished by the truck rather than the reverse occurrence.

Arriving home, she found Eric in a typical pose, slumped on the couch with a can of beer in one hand and a half eaten pork pie in the other. "You're home early" he said.

"You'll never believe what happened" she replied "I got fired this morning"

Valerie was used to Eric ignoring her stories when she arrived home from work, but this announcement gained his instant attention.

"Fired?" He screamed "How the hell could you get fired, don't you know very well that we need the money. What will we use to pay for my beer and pork pies?"

Vive la Resistance

"Anyone who joined the resistance needed a course in self judgement, or better still a prolonged stay in a mental institution" she was an old French lady of venerable appearance still in full possession of all her faculties except for the need for reading glasses, a fact which offended her sense of dignity, so she never read in public.

Not reading in public may seem like a relatively minor matter but it emphatically is not. Consider, if you will how often during our daily travails we are confronted with the need to read something. The simplest thing, such as the number of the swiftly approaching bus or the information banners on the Luas stations becomes a real challenge if your stiff necked pride won't let you don your specs to decipher them.

Consequently, a whole new set of skills is needed to get by when faced with such obstacles.

However enough of this chat about being ocularly challenged, we were talking about her rather strange statement about underground movements. She was in a particularly strong position to discourse on this subject as she had spent her teenage years as a fully paid up member of the Marquis, the French resistance movement.

Early in the German occupation of La Belle France her father and older brother had been snatched by the Gestapo whilst innocently enjoying a quiet glass of wine in the rather dingy cafe in the town square. They were never seen again.

Needless to state this had a catastrophic effect on the young girl. She contacted all the relevant authorities seeking news of her relatives but all professed complete ignorance of their whereabouts. Finally, she was called aside by the Mayor of the town and advised that if she didn't stop raising trouble, she might find herself disappeared too. He went on to suggest an alternative pursuit. She could strike a blow for freedom by joining the resistance and blowing the bejesus out of German convoys.

What right minded young girl could turn down such an opportunity? Very soon she became the most skilled bomb maker in Southern France and gained a reputation which was a rallying call to the oppressed youth of the nation. By the end of the war she has been responsible for the deaths of some one hundred and fifty German soldiers, and some French civilians, but hey, you can't make omelettes without breaking eggs, now can you?

When the fog of war had evaporated, however, the piper came demanding payment. The huge hype of being constantly on the run and the peaks and troughs of terror of imminent danger around every corner disappeared instantly and normal human behaviours returned once again to demand normality.

Evette, for that was her name, found this shift difficult, if not impossible, to accommodate. Having attempted suicide on a number of occasions she spent a long period of time in an institution, high in the Alps, being treated for profound depression.

Hound of Hell

I was lookin' out me back door, quietly mindin' me own business, enjoyin' the early spring days lengthenin' when what do ye think came into view.

Yer not goin' te believe me, but a very big, very shaggy hound with satanic red eyes and huge slaverin' teeth an' a spiky collar came boundin' over me neighbours fence and made a mad drive towards me.

Needless to state, I was a bit put out by this carry on. I mean, it's not every evenin' that the devils guard dog arrives in me garden. Now me garden is no great shakes at the best of times, but this bleeding canine had paws as big as Muhammad Ali's boxing gloves, with claws like cutthroat razors and he wasn't doin' me lawn much good, I can tell you.

I looked over me shoulder, casual like, ye know, not to excite the beast but to me considerable shock and distress, the back door was firmly shut and through the kitchen winda I could see me immediate superior pilin' up chairs and tables against the inside of it. So no escape that way.

Turnin' back I found the animal stood about five feet away from me, steam comin' from his nostrils and the hair on the nape of his neck standin' on end. I was, if truth be told, a little bi anxious about me position in this whole affair. I'm not mad keen on dogs at the best of times and this yolk wasn't improvin' matters any.

"There, there, Fido" I crooned softly in me best 'let's all by pals together' voice. "No need to be gettin' all imbrangled now, is there?. We can settle this like gentlemen"

And we did, down the boozer, him with a lovely juicy hambone and me with a nice creamy pin

Jimmy Choo's

Maria had just spent €700.00 on a pair of shoes, one pair of shoes, what had she been thinking of?

"As a matter of absolute fact" Said Maria "I hadn't been thinking of anything except, here's this darling pair of Jimmy Choo's just sitting here waiting for me to come through the door. I mean, look at them, aren't they the darlingest things you've ever seen.?"

"I have no wish to rain on anybody's parade, but they just look like a pair of shoes to me. I know I'm a man and therefore culpably unaware of the finer distinctions between one pair of lady's shoes and another but really, when Hardy comes to Hardy, as our northern brethren might be heard to say it's just something to keep the soles of your feet from scraping the ground. Or am I missing something" George was brave, but it must be admitted a few spoons short of a full set of cutlery.

"You are an unfeeling brute" Maria wept copiously "How can anyone call themselves a discriminating individual and still fail to appreciate the sublime beauty of these delicately crafted examples of the cobbler's art?"

"I give up" she turned and stormed out of the room.

George turned to his brother Fred who had been a silent onlooker to this passage of words "What did I say that's got her in a tizzwozz now?" He queried

"I despair of you" Said Fred "If you had two mouths you would spend most of your life with one foot in each of them. How long have you been married anyway? Twenty two years isn't it? I suppose if she ask does her bum look big in this dress you'd just answer honestly too? She's just spent €700.00 on a bloody pair of shoes and your response is to go into a spake about how all they're supposed to do is to keep her soles off the ground. How thick are you anyway?"

"Next time" Said George sulkily "I'll just keep my opinions to myself then. All I seem to do is get myself into trouble. I'll just give the old No Comment thing so"

"Carry on like that Bro, and there might very well not be a next time" Said Fred as he left the house and abandoned George to the tender mercies of his embittered wife.

An Antique Chair

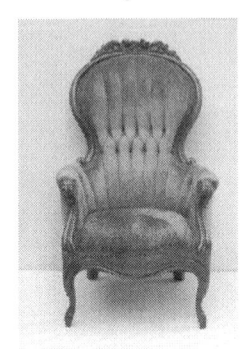

The song on the radio set me up. I should have known better, but I've always been a sucker for a smoothly delivered message, especially a musical one.

My relatives have all, at one time or another accused me of being always ready to jump in feet first without checking either the depth or temperature of the water, Whether that water was real or metaphorical so on the day after hearing "Granny had left me her old armchair" I set off on a buying spree in all the nearby auction rooms.

My quest was exclusively for old armchairs, not necessarily antique, old was to be good enough. With one stipulation, they should be generously upholstered and cheap. The idea being that on average there must be some treasure down the back of at least some of these abandoned pieces of furniture.

In my deluded state of mind, I figured that if I managed to find at least ten Euros worth of money in every tenth chair and if I didn't pay more than fifty cents per chair then I would, as the saying goes, be quids in.

Soon my small flat was totally packed with half dismembered chairs, with stuffing drifting out onto the landing every time I opened the door. Funnily enough by the time I had disembowelled my twentieth chair I had only managed to amass a half crown, fifteen farthings, three dozen mismatched buttons and a desiccated mouse corpse.

It dawned on me that my get rich scheme was, like many of my previous attempts doomed to ignominious failure. Not only that but a thunderous knocking on my door revealed upon opening it, my landlord and a burly fire officer, at least in his big boots and high fireman's helmet he looked burly.

Within an extremely short space of time I found myself outside on the pavement surrounded by a heap of broken furniture and all of my personal belongings distributed on top.

With scraps of conversation from my erstwhile neighbours like "Crazy loon" and "Mad as a hatter" ringing in my ears I plodded wearily away, dragging my assorted bits and bobs behind me and reflecting bitterly on my sainted mother's words "Don't believe what you hear on the radio, only believe what you see with your own eyes, and only believe half of that"

Loser

Gerald was tired of losing, he was determined he wasn't going to lose again so he decided he just wouldn't compete anymore.

Unfortunately for his grandiose plan, life wasn't prepared to agree with his wimpish ambitions. Life itself constantly throws challenges at all of us and we needs must compete on some level, like it or lump it. There is no get out clause.

Early morning and our gallant hero woke up with a thundering headache, probably brought on by his over indulgence in fifteen year old Irish Whisky last night. In line with his decision regarding non-competition he decided to give the whole day a miss. This might seem like a simple enough plan but in carrying it out his options were severely limited.

First off there was the headache, accompanied by a raging thirst and the need to check in with the office to explain his absence from work.

Groaning dismally, he struggled out of bed and stumbled down to the kitchen, pausing on the way to pick up his iPad in order to send an email to his employer. He didn't feel that he was up to a telephone conversation just yet, especially one which might just turn confrontational, given that this was the fifth Monday in a row that he was calling in to report sick.

Plugging in the kettle and contemplating the noise involved in buttering his toast he opted for sending the email while waiting for the cacophony in his head to subside. Opening his iPad, he was assaulted by an almighty trumpet blast, he had forgotten to turn down the volume after his nephew had finished viewing the WWF website and the volume was set to full blast.

      Cringing and turning the volume off he was amazed to note that he had a new email. This rarely happened to him. He had no friends or acquaintances, belonged to no clubs, associations, not even a writers group and he certainly had no time for social media in all its multifarious forms, so incoming emails were as scarce as hen's teeth.

      Even more astonishing was the content of the mail. YOU HAVE WON €2M, it screamed at him. This is odd, He thought,

      "I've never won anything in my life, I'm the original born loser. How could I have won €2M. I didn't even buy a lottery ticket, it must be a mistake, maybe the message is for some other Gerald. No, it's addressed to me at bornloser@gmail.com so it must be for me"

      "I know, I'll just click on the attachment and check it out"

Tough Love

For love it is pleasein'
And love it is teasin'
And love is a treasure wherever you go,
But as love grows older,
Sure love grows colder,
And it fades away like the morning dew.

Love exploits coincidence, is it mine?

Love me arse, I wouldn't give you a sop of hay for all the mouldy love stories in the world, and there's nothing coincidental about it either.

Long, long ago when I was a mere stripling I was bedazzled by a strapping girl from the banks of the Corrib in Galway.

She had hair as black as Satan's heart, eyes as blue the fabled cerulean sea and a figure designed by God to drive men mad with lust.

Sadly, for me, she had a heart as hard as the famous Cullinan Diamond and a mercenary nature as rapacious as the inner cohort of the bankers at the end of the Tiger Economy era.

For three glorious weeks we strutted around the City of the Tribes as though we were Lord and Lady of all we surveyed. The doors of each and every society matron were thrown open to us and we were welcomed with open arms in every drinking joint and night club within fifty miles of that benighted town.

Sadly, and realistically, inevitably, the money ran out. This may have been predictable but in my defence I should point out that my father, God rest his soul, was the owner of a vast property empire, with assets as far apart as the Russian Republic and Beijing in China. He, like many others of his ilk was caught with his metaphorical trousers down when the famous bubble burst and he found himself namanated and spectacularly bust. He went softly into that good night, despite the advice given by John Donne.

Seeking consolation for my new found woes on the ample bosom of my lady love I was devastated to hear her voice wafting over her shoulder as she sashayed out the door

"Good luck, loser" she said.

Rock'n'Roll to me and Billy Joel

Entering for American Idol may not have been the brightest thing I'd ever done, but who knew it would turn out like it did in the end.

It all began on a wet Wednesday afternoon in the Candy Cafe. I was sitting there, minding my own business, enjoying a cappuccino and a ham and cheese panini, or should that be a panino? Whatever lost in my iPad I took no notice of my surroundings until I felt a hand on my shoulder and heard a familiar voice in my ear "Hey bud, I've been looking everywhere for you. Where the hell have you been keeping yourself?" Looking up I saw Billy Joel, not that Billy Joel, his distant cousin from Ballyfermot towering over me. I use the term towering because in his case it was particularly apt. He stands six foot four in his stocking feet and he weighs in at twenty two stone.

"You know you're always going on about breaking into show business and writing hit songs and stuff, well I know a guy in the States who can get us on American Idol. So pack your bags and your iPad and let's go" He was deadly serious, I've known him since God was a boy and he has never been known to crack a joke.

"Don't be bloody stupid" I replied "You don't just get off a plane and go on American Idol. There's auditions and stuff. Any way you never told me you knew anyone in America, never mind someone who could get us on the telly"

"See now" he said "That's the advantage of having a name. This guy in the States seems to think I'm the real Billy Joel, you know the singer like, and he's under the impression that I've been hiding out in Ireland for the past couple of years. Seemingly the real deal is missing or something. Something to do with gambling or drug debts, I can't keep up with all that celeb stuff. Anyway, he's got a spot booked for Billy on American Idol and he's sent me the tickets. So, are you on or not?"

"But we'll be sussed the minute we rock up at the studio. Everyone in the world knows what Billy Joel looks like and we'd be like Mutt and Jeff. We'd never pull it off" despite my denial I still felt a tingle of excitement at the prospect, after all who gets a shot at American Idol right out of the blue?

In the event my doubts were proved only too accurate. We were apprehended at the studio gates, thrust into a police car, charged with impersonating a celebrity, ejected from the States and sent home in disgrace.

But it's still rock'n'roll to me and Billy Joel.

Accidental Arsonist

It really, really wasn't his fault, or so he insisted. In fairness it must be asked, Why wouldn't he use a bicycle pump to poke the fire? The pump was near at hand and the fact that it was made of an incredibly combustible plastic wasn't immediately obvious to his childish eyes.

It's incredible combustibility became very obvious within a nanosecond of it's introduction to the glowing coals in the old black range.

At this point the sublime began to morph into the ridiculous, you see there was a clothesline suspended over the range just under the mantelpiece and suspended from this line were several articles of clothing, referred to by all in the house as "smalls" or to be somewhat formal about it underclothes of both sexes, if clothes can be so described.

Discovering that he now held in his hand a flaming brand, throwing out bright golden flames like a blow torch, he did what any normal person might do. He waved it about frantically in a vain attempt to extinguish the flames. His efforts, well meaning as they were, were not successful. In point of fact the more he waved, the brighter flared the torch.

Now frantic he discovered, to his horror that the entire line of "Smalls" was blazing merrily. Behind him in the crowded kitchen of the red brick terraced house a huge hubbub arose as his extended family, whose main preoccupation had been waiting for the dinner to be placed on the table, commenced to shout suggestions and exhortations about the best way to deal with this conflagration.

"Pull the line down" Shouted one

"Throw some water on it" Was the advice from another

"Smother it with a wet rag" came yet another suggestion.

Meanwhile the unfortunate arsonist, visited by a blinding flash of wisdom, shoved the remainder of the pump into the fire, tore the "smalls" off the line and, ably assisted by his older brother stamped the fire out on the grate.

To this day he is not fond of cycling.

Airy Castles

Building castles in the air is not as easy as it sounds, especially when there are naysayers around every corner just waiting to carp and criticise at any and all opportunities and none.

Still, nothing ventured, nothing gained. Here goes,

The actual practice of building these airy structures is a complex one and can very easily be misunderstood. They require a vast amount of emotional and spiritual input and they are, at best, fragile and ephemeral. The slightest negative vibration is likely to send them toppling to their doom, causing sadness and distress to both their constructor and to his appreciative followers.

Many times, my fabrications have been shattered by the ridicule of uneducated, and uneducable morons pronouncing their ill formed opinions, frequently when the structure in question is in its nascent state. Perhaps if they had the good manners and patience to wait until its completion, they might, however unlikely that might is, appreciate the finished article. But no, the great unwashed must needs stick their three pence worth in at the most inappropriate and most delicate moments of the creative process.

In consequence, I have decided that nobody shall be present when I am actively engaged in the constructive process. My designs will not be exposed to the cold blasts of the hostile world until each and every jot and tittle of the project has been slotted into its assigned place in the overall scheme of things.

Only when my masterpiece is completed will I consent to it being shown to a carefully selected group of like minded enthusiasts for their delectation and pleasure.

The great unwashed can kiss me arse after that.

Pearly Gates

Eric died like he had lived, quietly and without fuss. Truth to tell he had made very little impact on his surroundings in life. He had done reasonably well in school and college, failed in his few half hearted attempts at meeting members of the opposite sex and soldiered on for forty five years in an anonymous office in a back street.

Arriving at the pearly gates he was confronted by the archangel Gabriel on the right hand side and his fellow archangel Michael on the left. As he approached these two august personages, somewhat diffidently, he was astonished to find them brushed aside by Saint Peter himself.

"Come in, Eric, come in" St Peter boomed. He tended to boom when excited. "We have been preparing for your arrival for a long time" He went on "It's rare, even unprecedented to have someone with a record like yours arrive on our doorstep"

Eric was all a bit befuddled by this level of attention. He had always shunned the limelight in life and couldn't understand what all the fuss was about now.

"Have I done something wrong?" He queried "Maybe I should have come to another gate. I'm sorry if I've offended some protocol, if you'd be good enough to point me in the right direction I'll get out of your hair"

"No, no, no" St Peter was booming again "You are a very unusual person. In fact I can confidently say that you are unique. We've looked at your slate, you know, the balance we keep of the good and the bad you've done in life and we find that, whilst on the positive side there's not much to shout about, on the negative side your slate is totally clean. There is not one unfriendly act or thought, no lustful or carnal ideas marked down, you've never gone on the bus without paying the exact right fare and, all in all, you've led an exemplary life.

"More than all that you are the first person in recorded history to have a completely clean slate on arrival here"

"It wasn't down to any effort on my part" Eric was reluctant to accept any kudos for his exemplary behaviour "It was always my way to stay out of trouble as far as possible. I'm not one of those people who think that rules are there to be broken"

"Well, whether or which, you are our number one guest today and all you have to do is ask and anything will be granted to you, and I mean anything" With this Peter offered a salacious wink.

"Actually, this might be difficult" Eric hesitated

"When I said anything" Peter growled, "I meant anything, spit it out man"

"I shouldn't say this at this time, but I'd really like to take a tour of hell" Said Eric diffidently

"A tour of hell?" St Peter thundered, merely booming didn't seem to meet the case "I'm not sure that's even possible. Nobody has ever asked for it before. There's just no protocol for it. We normally keep ourselves to ourselves and let the other lot look after themselves. There's not a lot of communication between the two realms, if you understand me"

"But surely there's a hotline? Even the Americans and the Russians had one of those and they weren't exactly bosom buddies, now were they?"

Rabbit Hole

Once upon a time and a very long time it was ago too, Jimmy fell down a rabbit hole.

The hole was somewhat unusual in that it had appeared, unannounced, in his living room floor.

Jimmy had been about to set up his Xbox to play some Fortnite with his buddy Paul. But so focused was he on the game that he didn't notice the emergence of an enormous hole, bathed in a pink glow, in his floor.

Oddly enough, when, as might have been predicted, he fell into the hole he didn't go hurtling downward. In fact, his fall was more like the drift of a Jinny Joe rather than the plummet of a lump of coal.

The fall, or drift, if you would prefer, seemed to take a very long time and Jimmy was thoroughly bored by the time he arrived at his destination. He found it was lined with large, fluffy, pink, cushions so that his landing was soft and pleasant.

Imagine his astonishment when, at the bottom of the hole, he was greeted by a reception committee of paper people. These were two dimensional people, separated by gender, holding hands in threes. Jimmy quickly decided that they were made of notepaper.

Climbing off the cushions presented its own challenge however, as he found it difficult to maintain his balance, much to his embarrassment in front of the paper people. However, with more of a controlled stumble than a dignified walk, he stood erect before the welcoming committee.

As he finally dusted himself down the paper people, who seemed pleased to see him, if a bit apprehensive, commenced to sing, in total harmony in high treble voices "I can't do my Belly Bottom Button Up"

Jimmy thought that the song didn't make a lot of sense, but he was reluctant to say so. His mother had always told him "If you can't say something nice, don't say anything at all" Also he was afraid he might upset the Skinnies, as he had decided to call them, if he came across as hyper critical.

As the song came to an end, one of the girl Skinnies approached him and said "You look a bit strange. Where did you come from and how did you make the big pink hole?"

"What do you mean, where do I come from. I'm from the real world. Where do you guys come from and how come you can walk and talk" Jimmy demanded indignantly.

"It might have escaped your notice" Chorused a trio of Skinnies in high treble harmony "But this is our place, We don't "come from" anywhere. We're from here. You're the outsider. So, it would be more civil of you to answer our questions, first and then we'll answer yours"

"This is just on the weird side of bizarre" snapped Jimmy "But I'm from up top" he pointed upwards "I was at home in my house when this hole appeared in my floor. I didn't notice it until I fell in and landed here"

"Wow" carolled the trio "That's very odd, but you're quite funny looking. You're three dimensional for one thing and you're coloured too. We've never seen anything like you before. Tell you what, why don't we take you to our leader?"

"To your leader? You have a leader? What's he like, is he made of cardboard?" Jimmy said with a sarcastic sneer.

"There's no need to be like that" Trebled the trio "It's nice to be nice! If you can't say anything nice you should keep your trap shut" and turning on Jimmy they gave him three kicks on his right shin.

Have you ever been kicked on the shin by a trio of paper people? I bet you haven't. I bet think it doesn't hurt. Well let me tell you it hurts like hell. Have you ever gotten a paper cut; it hurts like hell. Well the kicks were a million times worse.

Jimmy woke up in his garden with ants, whose nest he had been lying on, biting his shins.

"God" the mumbled," That was more a nightmare than a dream"

Snow White

The wrappers from three pregnancy tests lay discarded on the vanity unit.

Grumpy stormed into the room, "Who's the father? He roared. "I can't leave you for five minutes but you're getting yourself into trouble. And another thing, why three tests? For God's sake don't tell me that you were stravaging' with three of them. Your dear sainted Grandmother always said that you were destined to go bad, I'm only glad that she didn't live to see the shame you've brought on this house, that's all"

"Ah, will you go easy on the poor girl" Entreated Doc "She's only a slip of a girl. Someone must have taken a mean advantage of her, that's all"

Sleepy stumbled into the room, rubbing the sleep out of his eyes "What's all the racket, a person can't get a wink of sleep around here, but someone is making a row. Will yiz all quiet down and let me get back to sleep" and turning he headed back to his bedroom.

"Well one thing we can be sure of, it wasn't him anyway. Sure he wouldn't get out of his own way. Now c'mon, fess up, who's the father or fathers, whichever the case may be" Grumpy tended to get, well, grumpy when he was disturbed.

Happy was cheerfully sitting in the corner, saying nothing and imbibing a large tankard of beer with a smile as big as today and tomorrow on his face.

Bashful said hesitatingly "Why is Happy looking so pleased with himself, it couldn't be that he's the culprit, could it?"

"Ah choo" An enormous sneeze was all that Sneezy was able to contribute to the matter,

"Bless you" Said Dopey

"Jeez, you're all a bunch of old women" Cried Snow White "The tests weren't for me, they were for Bambi the deer and Timor the mouse and Thumper the rabbit, apparently they had a bit of a rave on Saturday night and things may have gotten out of hand, just a bit. Now will you all finish your dinners and get back to work, hi, ho, hi, ho, hi, ho"

Face Time

"When I am looking at your face, do I look at myself or you?" He was, in fairness as drunk as a skunk when he said this. I have a long standing agreement with myself that I will not engage in sensible conversation with people who are non compos mentis, as they say.

So, I replied "The Barbary apes of Gibraltar are the only wild apes on the European continent"

He took a long pull at his pint and mumbled "What has that got to do with anything? I always say if you can't say anything nice, you shouldn't say anything at all"

"I'm in full and complete agreement with you on that" I replied "County Roscommon is one third bogland. Not a lot of people, except for Roscommoners, know that"

He was now gazing with some puzzlement into his half full glass as if he might find enlightenment therein "I was talking about looking into people's faces" He growled "What are you going on about, Barbary apes and Roscommon bogland, you are not making sense" he looked seriously put out by my apparent insistence on talking in non sequiturs.

"Faces is it?" I demanded "What do you know about faces anyway, you have a face like a mad arse yourself. If I had a face like yours I'd stay in bed in the morning and I wouldn't move out except on moonless nights when it's cloudy"

Throwing back the remains of his drink he rose unsteadily to his feet and made his stumbling way out of the bar. As he went he was heard to mutter "I should have known better than to get into conversation with a creative writer"

Paddy Paragon

Paddy was the original paragon of all the virtues. He went to ten o'clock mass every day of his life since his early retirement. Prior to that his sister, an unclaimed treasure whose sole function in life was to give Paddy grief about everything and nothing, was fond of saying that he was the only man in Dublin who was paid to go to mass.

During his years of paid employment, not to confuse it with work, in Dublin Corporation, Paddy was first into his office in Marrowbone lane, signed the book with a graceful flourish and then left to go to mass in the Oratory in the Coombe Maternity Hospital, a short walk from his "Workplace"

All during his life he had contributed to a raft of worthy causes, was a member of The Legion of Mary, the Pioneer Total Abstinence Association and the Third Order of St Francis.

Image his annoyance and dismay when having died, as he would have put it, In A State of Grace, he found himself in a non-celestial environment, surrounded by downcast individuals who looked as though they had never done a charitable deed in their lives. Worse than that they were all in the process of being driven towards a great wide open brazen door with flames curling around the lintels. Their drivers were small, red creatures, armed with tridents which packed a severe wallop when driven into ones buttocks, as Paddy found to his mortification when he attempted to remonstrate with these creatures.

Finally, with a tremendous squeeze the entire crowd, demons and humans alike burst through the brazen doors. Here Paddy determined that enough was enough and facing up to an individual as red as the imps, but over seven feet tall from the cloven hoofs on his feet to the tips of his tiny horns.

"Here you" He adopted his Managers voice, the one he kept for the lesser mortals who worked for him in his glory days in the Corpo "I'm in the wrong place, you've gotten the wrong end of the stick. I'll have you know I'm on very good terms with the man above and I can assure you if you don't straighten this out tout sweet, you'll get a flea in your ear, so you will"

"Ah, listen to him will ya" Satan, for that's who it was cried "Like I never heard the auld 'I'm in the wrong place story before. Let me tell you, sonny boy, there are no mistakes made here. First off, your name goes to the big panjandrum in the sky above. His minions, ye know, the archangels and angels checks out their list. If yer not on it, yer out. And after that the only way is down, as they say. Then ye come down here and we don't take just anybody either, we have our standards, so we have"

"But there must be an appeals process" Said a disbelieving Paddy "I've lived an exemplary life and I demand that you send me back where I belong"

"See now, that's where yer wrong, we used to have an appeals process, but then Owen Keegan was put in charge and all that nonsense has been binned. Welcome to hell Paddy"

Glendalough

The plish plash of the oars as the boat approached should have been reassuring but, in fact, for some unknown reason shivers ran up my spine as the hair on the nape of my neck rose.

This expedition should have been a pleasant afternoon on the water with the lake water lapping and the sound of songbirds filling the drowsy summer air. Unfortunately, something had gone severely astray almost as soon as we set out in our inflatable kayak. As we paddled enthusiastically across the lake in search of St Kevin's bed, I noticed that we appeared to be a little too heavy in the bows. Things rapidly went from bad to worse as a thick and cloying mist descended on us with absolutely no visible points of reference to help with navigation.

Finding water seeping up my legs I decided to attempt to find a landing but with the ever thickening fog surrounding us my task was well nigh impossible. To my extreme relief I felt the grating of stones under our keel and letting out a gasp of relief I jumped out of the boat and dragged it up the shallow bank which had appeared almost miraculously.

My relief turned to apprehension as we beheld an extraordinary looking person looming out of the mist. He, it must be a he, I decided, as he had a long beard down to below the waist, called out in a loud voice "Begone from here you accursed strangers, no woman must defile this holy place of prayer and contemplation"

"St Kevin?" I stammered, "We're sorry to intrude on your meditations but we've become lost in the mist and our boat has sprung a leak. Could you please help us. My mobile phone seems to have gotten water into it and my companion has left hers in the car"

Strictly speaking I didn't really think he was St Kevin but dressed in animal skins, long beard and open sandals I figured that there was a good chance that he thought he was the sainted misogynist.

"The last female that I came upon here was Kathleen and I dropped her from a height into the bottomless lake, what makes you think I should treat you pair of ragamuffins any differently" this diatribe delivered while he brandished a scythe over his dishevelled head.

Just at this interesting juncture we heard the sound of an approaching boat. "Ahoy there" called the voice from the small craft, "We're just out for an afternoons rowing and we seem to have become somewhat lost. Are we anywhere near Sandycove, can you tell me? Buck Mulligan promised some tea and scones this afternoon and we'd hate to be late"

Duvet Day

It was going to rain all day, and there was nothing Samantha could do about it.

So, like any sensible person she banked up the fire, opened a box of Dairy Milk Chocolates and settled back to read the latest Mills and Boon offering.

Between the heat of the fire, the soporific effect of the chocolate and the blockbuster she soon nodded off into the arms of Morpheus.

Entering a dream state she soon found herself involved as a central character in a chick lit drama of epic proportions, meeting a tall dark, handsome fellow, falling madly in love with him, eloping to Elba, in order to escape her wicked uncle who had lascivious deigns on her maidenly virtue, and eventually finding out that the light of her life was not the shining knight she had envisioned but was a bounder, a cad, and had only tipped his cap at her in order to gain control of her not inconsiderable fortune.

Samantha, however, was made of sterner stuff, even in a dream state, and had kept tight control of her own finances ever since her older brother had finagled her out of three pence, a sum which was, to her certain knowledge still outstanding some forty five years later.

Having discovered her Lothario's vile intentions by reading his emails she decided to give him the old heave ho. He, however had other ideas and threatened to reveal to the world her shameful secret, too shameful to include in this piece as it is for a mixed audience.

She now found herself in the proverbial cleft stick, should she proceed with her plans to dump him or resort to sterner measures?

It wasn't really that difficult a choice. He had, in common with herself an inordinate fondness for chocolate bonbons. Many quarrels had arisen between them over the distribution of contents of the bonbon box during their brief liaison, with harsh words being exchanged when the box was found, empty, under the living room couch. An occurrence which happened, coincidently more often when Samantha was home alone, than otherwise.

She procured, by devious use of her feminine wiles, a quantity of ricin, a chemical which once ingested is instantly fatal. Using the recommended safety precautions, she injected several bonbons with the poison and replaced the randomly on the box, leaving them in a prominent position where they would fall easily into Lothario's greedy grasp.

Sadly, for Samantha, Lothario had come up with a similar scheme, planting a poisoned box of bonbons convenient to her hand. After one more flaming row, she flounced out of the room and grabbing up her box of sweets retired to bed, saying as she went "The spare room is made up for you"

Hidden Treasure

Digging through the attic last week Joe found a carefully wrapped box behind the numerous, now rarely used suitcases, nobody takes suitcases on planes anymore, they're too damn heavy and if travelling by car any old sports bag will suffice.

At any rate to return to the mysterious well wrapped box, he decided to open the wrapping and check out the contents. The parcel was entombed in several black plastic bags, tightly sealed with a particularly stubborn tape and once through this obstacle four layers of tissue paper followed.

Now in a fever of impatience Joe tore the tissue off and discarded it then gazed thunderstruck at the treasure revealed.

"Dear God" he thought, "I really believed that if I didn't get this back in 1986 that the world would come to a shuddering halt. How did it come to be up here, and wrapped up like the Crown Jewels too? I'm quite certain that I never laid eyes on this before"

"Maura" he shouted down the stairs, "Can you come up here for a minute? I've got something you might have some ideas about"

Maura climbed to attic stairs, protesting at every step, she wasn't over keen on climbing the rickety contraption which Joe had constructed many years ago in his DIY phase. He wasn't very good at DIY then and the stairs had not improved over the passage of time since.

"You are a doddering old fart" she said with a twinkle in her eye as he reached down to assist her through the trapdoor. "What are you on about now?"

"I found this parcel here behind the suitcases and I opened it up. Look what was inside" He said, peevishly displaying his treasure trove.

"I wanted one of these back in 1986 and I would have given my eye teeth for it then. I must have dropped hints for months around birthdays, Christmas time and anniversaries but it never materialised. So, what's it doing here then?"

"I remember, I bought it in January in the sales for your birthday back then, and I hid it in the attic, but, you remember, that was the year you spent your birthday in the Coronary Care Unit in Beaumont. I forgot all about it. Fancy you finding it now. Never mind, I'm sure you'd like it for your birthday this year instead"

"No bloody fear, I'm gone right off the whole idea, give it to your brother and get me a nice single malt whiskey instead"

The Bank Managers Dilemma

Personally, I thought that there was more than a hint of sarcasm in the letter. After all I am the bank manager and it's my occasional unhappy task to write to people, sometimes numerous times, in order to have them discharge their duty to repay their loans.

I know very well that times are hard, and that old man adversity has many of our customers firmly gripped by the hasp of their arse, but that hardly warrants discourtesy and disdain from the customers. This particular gentleman, being seriously in arrears, has been in receipt of a great number of letters from me, without response until this rather juvenile missive.

However, reading on

Dear Mr Bank Manager,

I think it's very nice of you to keep writing to me, on account of me being a stranger to you and all.

It is, however, my melancholy misfortune to further rain on your already sodden day, but I must inform you that you have about as much chance of squeezing anything more out of me as the proverbial small dog has in hell.

In the first place I have lost my very lucrative position in the prestigious stockbroking firm of Brand, McAddam, Sweeney and Partners. I had been led to believe that I would be offered a partnership, but unfortunately the recession struck, and I found myself, penniless, on the street.

My dear lady wife, upon being informed of this tragic occurrence, immediately and without forewarning, emptied our joint bank account and fled the jurisdiction with her personal trainer, a young giant with no prospects and less intelligence, though, to be fair a very good looking lad.

Hard on the heels of this catastrophe my long time friend and confidante, Maximilian, my Great Dane, died of a mysterious canine illness, leaving me without any form of companionship whatsoever.

Last but not least, it emerged that the malicious bitch had actually sold the house over my head and I'm now homeless.

Consequently, I cannot adequately express my gratitude for your continued correspondence, and I hope that it will not prove to be a burden on your time to send me my regular communication from time to time.

Yours in penury,

Joe Soap,

PS, the keys to the Porsche are in the post.

What's a poor bank manager to do?

Puncture

He woke up with a pounding headache. "Where the bloody hell am I?" he muttered, wincing at the flash of pain which his voice prompted in his poor head.

"Sure, you're in Connemara" said a little man dressed in a green coat and black tight pants.

"Connemara?" The aching headed one queried "How did I get here; I was on my way to a very important meeting in the City of London. I seem to remember something to do with a bicycle, but nothing else"

"Ah, well it's like this yer honour" Said the little man in a thick brogue "My cousin Sean Og MacGroarty was in London on one of his visits to the Bank of England, just to check on his deposits there, don't ye know. He likes to travel everywhere on his bike and he's not the most observant road user in the world. In fact, he may have imbibed a trifle more than the prescribed limit of the Uisce Beatha with his breakfast stirabout. Anyway, you seem to have become embrangled with the bike, and thinking it was himself that was in it, the foolish machine brought you home. It wouldn't be the first time ye know"

"You're havin' me on, aren't you" demanded Achinhead. "Next thing you'll be telling me that I got run over by a Leprechaun on a bike in Throgmorton Street and woke up in Connemara, pull the other one, why don't you?"

"You need to be a little bit less obstreperous with yer tongue, young man" Said the little man "Around here we don't much like people bad mouthing the little people. It tends to be bad for their health, if ye get me drift"

"Listen" the sufferer was getting more and more fed up with this conversation "All I want at this moment is to get something for my sore head and to find my way back to my important meeting in the City. Can you help me with that?"

"It's not beyond the bounds of possibility" Said the little man "But there's a couple of things we need to straighten out first. Number one, where's me cousin Sean Og? And who is goin' to pay for fixing the puncture in the bike? Last but not least could you spare a couple of coppers for something to drink, I'm demented with the drought, so I am"

A telephone call

"It's bleedin' awful cold" Mumbled monkey number one through his hands which were clamped over his mouth.

"What'd he say" asked Monkey number two whose hearing was massively impaired due to the obstruction presented by his hands over his ears. "I can't hear a bloody thing, there must be something wrong with the acoustics in here. Anyway, how are we expected to hear him if he insists on mumbling through his hands like that?"

Monkey number three was frantically trying to avoid taking part in this fragmented conversation whilst blindfolded by his hands. In his mind the intellectual capacity of his two companions was sadly lacking and far beneath his lofty standards.

Suddenly the comparative peace of the arctic tundra on which some sadist had deposited them was broken by the shrill tones of an iPhone banging out the theme from the Lone Ranger.

Number three said, in a condescending tone "Would one of you kindly answer that. It can't be for me. This is my contemplative hour, everyone who knows me knows not to call me at this time. It's just not done, anyway, I can't see the damn thing"

Number one mumbled something incomprehensible while number three demanded "What's going on guys, c'mon tell me. You guys know that I'm audio-logically challenged"

Cursing a blue streak number two scrabbled around and finding the offending instrument, picked it up with his foot and barked into it "Who's calling? You should know better than to interrupt my contemplative hour. Speak quickly and concisely so that I can get back to my exercises"

The voice at the other end said "I'm terribly sorry, I must have the wrong number. I was looking to confirm a pickup of three monkeys for delivery back to Africa. Sorry about that, Arctic Taxis out" brr, brr.

Philosophical Musings

"That's just the sort of claptrap I'd expect from a bunch of so called creative writers" Snapped Homer "Never is he more alone than when he does nothing, and never does he do nothing when he is active by himself. What a load of codswallop, from some dude called Cato, or something"

"It reminds me of the time when we were barred from Mo's for not paying our tabs. Me and Lenny and Carl were forced to sit in my car, sucking sachets of ketchup and discussing Wittgenstein when Chief Wiggum came up and ticketed us for loitering with intent. How ridiculous is that? We don't have a tent that's big enough for all three of us to loiter in and anyway we were in my car, it's not much of a car, but a tent it ain't"

"That philosophical stuff would be right up Lisa's alley. She goes in for all that stuff, I swear I have no idea where she got her brains from, but she certainly leaves me dragging my keister in the dust when she gets going."

"Bart now, he's a different kettle of fish. What you see is what you get with him, that's for sure. He's a right royal pain in the butt but your never left to wonder what he's on about. When he shouts cowabunga dude or eat my shorts, you might be driven to maniacal rage, but you know exactly where he's coming from"

"The little one, what's her name? Oh yeah, Maggie. She really doesn't have much to say for herself but she's only a baby really. Mind you she did shoot that old geezer Mr Burns, but he deserved it. Other than that, she hasn't done anything of note recently"

"Then there's Marge. What can I say about Marge? She is my sun and moon, but she sure can get her dander up when she's roused. She's a little myopic about Bart and she thinks the sun, moon and stars shine out of Lisa. How she lives with me I don't know but I sure am glad to have her on my side"

"Anyway, you can take that philosophical creative writers bull and stuff it where the sun don't shine if you want my opinion!"

She Reaps a Cruel Revenge

"Some thieving bastard has stolen my slippers" Snarled Grandma Kranky in her usual disagreeable, highly irritating whine. "If they're not brought to me instantly I'll wreak havoc on everybody in the house, without fear or favour"

Crouched down behind the high backed chair in which she was, as usual, ensconced I chuckled quietly to myself. " She'll never guess it was me" I thought as I munched on my fruit and nut chocolate bar.

I really should have known better, Granny Kranky has never been bested, by anybody, in living memory, mostly her own memory since she was, by far and away, the oldest living person in our town, or any other town, so far as we knew.

Silently enjoying the delicious sweet taste of the chocolate and the discreet crunch of the hazelnuts trapped in it I suddenly felt an excruciating pain in the top of my head.

"Come out of there" the old witch grated as she pulled me upright by my boyish curls "I know it was you, and even if it wasn't then you deserve punishment, if not for stealing my slippers, then for something else. Small boys should be beaten on sight, if they are not coming out of mischief, they're going into it"

"It wasn't me Grandma Kranky" I whinged "I wasn't even in the house when it happened"

"When what happened?" The venerable old lady demanded. "I was asking about my slippers. What other tricks have you been up to you spawn of the devil?"

"It's the chocolate bar, Grandma, isn't it? I found it on the road, I swear"

"Chocolate bar?" She screeched, spittle flying into my face "You've not only hidden my slippers, but you've eaten the fruit and nut chocolate bar I've been saving for a treat for myself. The curse of the seven snotty orphans of Glendalough and Clonmacnoise on you. You'll roast in hell for your duplicity and thievery"

Saying this she reached for her walking stick which was always laid convenient to her hand against the frequent necessity to physically chastise some errant small boy.

Faced with her cruel revenge, I spied the errant slippers under the back of the high backed chair. "Hey Grandma" I cried "Here's your slippers, they were under your chair all the time"

"Ah thank the good Lord for that, you're a good boy. What were we talking about before?"

Thank God for Alzheimer's!

Baked Treat

"I'm going to make an apple tart" Freddy said.

"Don't be so silly" his adoring life partner, Cecilia, said snappishly. "You never cooked in your life, you don't have any apples, you don't have any pastry or the wherewithal to make it with and even if you did have any of those things, you haven't the first blast of a notion as to where to start"

"That's what everyone told Napoleon Bonaparte when he set out to conquer the world" said Freddie "If he'd listened to all the naysayers, he would have stayed stuck as a corporal in an artillery battery all his life. Look what he accomplished"

Cecilia tossed her raven locks and sneering, said "And look where he finished up, on a rat infested island a million miles away from everybody and poisoned in his bed"

"Jeez Cecilia, I'm hardly going to be exiled to St Helena and poisoned in my bed if I attempt a little bakery. I know I've never done it before, but everybody should try something new every day, otherwise they'll just stultify"

"So, how do you propose to start"

"I'll start where everybody else starts, I'll google it and go on from there"

"Good luck with that. I'm going into town to look for that burnt orange sweater I've been searching for. Jenny said they've got something in Arnott's"

Some hours later she arrived home, tired, sweaterless and dispirited. As she opened the front door she was greeted with the most delicious smell of fresh baking.

In the kitchen Freddie was gazing at an apple tart, not just any apple tart but a work of artistic perfection.

"My god Freddie, I didn't think you had it in you" She enthused "It looks gorgeous, and the smell! Can I cut it? Did it take long to make?"

With a wry smile Freddie said "I looked it up on Google as I said, and I went to the shop and got the ingredients. I followed all Dr Googles instructions and it was an unmitigated disaster. In the end I went to the French patisserie on the corner and bought it. Tuck in doll"

Irises by the Pond

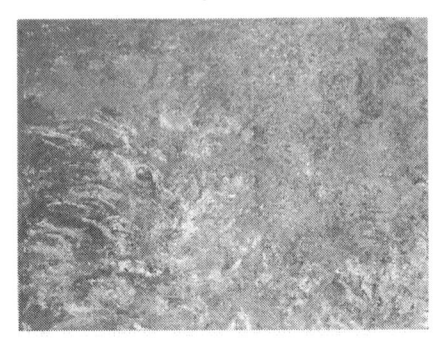

Claude Monet Irises by the Pond 1914-1917

"More and more people are refusing to obey the laws of the land" said Frances with a pugnacious and supercilious toss of her tawny locks. She was very proud of her tawny locks and never missed an opportunity to toss them whether such tossing was appropriate or not.

"That's just bullshit" retorted Billy "This land of ours is sinking under the weight of laws promulgated by our lords and masters which are totally ignored as soon as they are enacted. In fact, since penal times, and probably before, ignoring the law of the land is most likely the most popular sport in the country, even counting GAA, Soccer, Rugby and, latterly Cricket. There's just nothing new about it"

"How can you say such a thing?" Demanded she of the tawny locks "Tell me one law that's ignored by all and sundry"

"Tell me you haven't noticed the lines of cars parked with two and sometimes four wheels planted on footpaths the length and breadth of our fair city? How about the wholesale crashing of red lights pretty much everywhere you go in the country and where do you leave the universal jaywalking to be found on our highways and byways? and that's just the traffic laws" Billy paused to gather his breath.

"But that's not everyone, it's just the nasty bad mannered folks who are to be found all over the world. It's not unique to this land of saints and scholars" Frances demurred.

"Yeah, but the big difference here is that we invent new laws on a daily basis and the more we enact the less we enforce. It's a bit like Dublin City Council, the more services we farm out to private providers, the greater our property taxes. that's the Iron Law Of Diminishing Returns which some esteemed professor put forward, the more you put in, the less you get out, in plain language" Billy crowed, triumphantly.

"You make me sick with your negativity" Cried Frances "I'm off to watch the irises growing by the pond, that's a lot more uplifting than your constant whinging" And tossing her tawny locks in disdain, she stormed out.

Cloak and Dagger

Someone walks by your table, and drops a folded napkin, trying to be discreet. It is a note saying "Get out now, while you still can"

Sitting in my favourite restaurant and looking out at the frost shrouded trees in St Stephens Green I noticed a beautiful young lady, wearing a flattering red dress, threading through the tables in my direction. as she neared me I was struck by the way she never looked directly in my direction but seemed to focus on a spot over my right shoulder.

Still blithely ignoring me she walked by, exiting the room, leaving behind a scent of lily of the valley. Turning back to my perfectly cooked rare fillet steak I noticed a folded napkin lying on the floor almost at my toe.

Being, as I am, a confirmed tidier upper I reached down and retrieved the offending piece of paper. As I rolled it up preparatory to disposing of it in the recommended fashion my eye was drawn to some writing on it "Get out NOW, while you still can" screamed the note, written in scarlet lip gloss.

Well, a nod is as good as a wink to a blind horse, to quote the old saying so I hurriedly called for the bill and throwing a bundle of euros on the table I left precipitously. Outside on the steps of the premises I paused to draw a breath of cold, refreshing air. Suddenly a red car drew up to the pavement and the lady in red leaned over and called out the open passenger window "Don't just stand there, get in, we have very little time"

As I, with some trepidation, climbed into the car she slammed it into gear and streamed away from the curb with a squeal of tortured rubber "Were you followed?" she demanded, flicking her eye towards the rear view mirror.

"I'm not accustomed to this type of cloak and dagger carry on" I replied "How would I know if I was followed"

With a hollow laugh she cried "Stick with me and you'll know a lot more than you do now, that's if we survive the next couple of hours"

She Was Only Sixteen

She was only sixteen, only sixteen,
She was too young to fall in love,
And I was too young to know

Jenny found herself singing the song 'She was only sixteen' and humming it incessantly under her breath at all times and in all circumstances, both appropriate and not. We've all had the experience; the bloody thing sticks in the mind and won't let go.

After three days of being driven to the brink of despair by the repetitive lyrics and the unmemorable tune she frantically sought for something to distract her mind.

As she plodded through her daily chores a voice spoke from behind her left shoulder. "Hey" the man said on the radio "The clocks go back tomorrow. We'll get an extra hours lie in, cool huh?"

Feeling sorry for herself Jenny thought "The clocks go back? What does that matter to me, I'll probably be in the home for the bewildered by this time tomorrow with this blasted song going around and around. Maybe that's what I need, a spell in the looney bin, that might straighten me out. On second thought maybe I'll hold off on that option"

"I know, I won't put my clock back like everybody else. That should cause a bit of a blip in my life as I try to get along with the whole world an hour out of synch with me."

The next morning she was jolted, by the shrill noise of her alarm clock, out of her dream about a lovelorn seventeen year old boy, whinging desperately for his lost sweetheart. "Bloody hell, now I'm dreaming about it. This has to stop"

Rushing to catch her bus she was surprised to see that none of the usual gang were waiting for the number 46a as normal. Furthermore, looking up the long straight road she could see no sign of the approaching bus.

"Blast!" She muttered, "Don't tell me I missed the bloody thing. No, my watch says I'm five minutes early"

Suddenly it struck her "The clock, I never put it back, I'm an hour early for everything. When's the next bus due?"

Fiddling with the travel app on her iPhone she saw that she must wait another twenty five minutes for a bus. As she waited it suddenly dawned on her that she hadn't hummed the song for two whole minutes.

Unrequited Love

She had arthritis and headed off to Lanzarote every October.

Last year, however, her pet poodle, Arthritis, refused point blank to set foot outside the house once the days began to shorten.

"What's the problem, snookums?" She queried attempting tried and tested ruses to get the rat like hound to venture out. "Is it the big German Shepherd next door, sure he's just a big softie. You just watch, my little poodlums, I'll give him a big juicy bone to chew on and he won't even notice you passing his door" So saying she gathered Arthritis into her ample bosom and headed for the front door.

"Stop, stop, stop" Snarled Arthritis "It's nothing to do with the mutt next door. It's this insistence on going to landsagrotty every year, year after year. I'm fed up to the back teeth with sand, sun sea and all the rest. You go on to the hellhole if you must. I'm staying right here"

"My God, you spoke" She could hardly believe her ears. "I didn't know you could speak; we've been together for twelve years and you never spoke before. Why didn't you speak to me before?"

"Because I'm twelve years old and in dog years that equals about 84 years. I'm too old and long in the tooth to be trailing around the bars and beaches of Puerto del Carmen anymore. So just put that in your pipe and smoke it, I'm not going and that's that"

"Well then, where would you like to go instead? We can go anywhere you'd like you know, I thought you loved going to Lanzarote. You should have told me before this if you didn't like it"

"I want to go to Hollywood and meet Lassie" Arthritis replied "And by the way, what sort of a stupid name is Arthritis for a dog anyway"

"We can go to Hollywood, but I have to tell you that Lassie was a boy dog and he's long dead these forty years or more"

"Nooooo...."

Time Flies

"It's a chronsynclastic infundiblium" Said Professor Fergusson "Or if you want to be vulgar a flux capacitor"

"OK Prof" I replied "But what does it do?"

"Well to put it at its simplest it creates a temporal flux that allows me to travel through time" He said in a somewhat distracted voice.

"All due respect to you Prof, but you don't exactly seem to be jumping for joy here. I mean a time machine, Really? Like with a thing like that you could be the richest man in history, see all the pivotal moments of the past up close and personal. You know what I mean. But you seem to be a bit distracted. What gives"

"It doesn't only go back in time, it also goes forward too, but it does raise some moral and ethical dilemmas too. I could go forward and check out the Euromillions jackpot, then come back and buy a ticket with utter certainty that I'd win. But what about the people who wouldn't win because of my success? Or those whose winnings would be reduced if I only won a shared jackpot" his frown deepened as he spoke.

"It's well known that Homer Simpson is an Icon of mine" I said "and before today I would be in complete agreement with his contention that trying is the first step towards failure, but with this yoke you can eliminate any chance of failure

168

altogether. My god, you could be ruler of the world in the snap of a fingers" I was getting quite excited now "This is the greatest thing since hot buttered toast. Why don't we give it a go Prof?"

Assuming his professorial face he snapped "Haven't you been listening to a word I said? Messing with time would have consequences and it would take wiser minds than mine, and certainly yours to figure out how to navigate your way through the many and various issues that might easily trip you up if you went blithely crashing up and down the timelines. All things considered I'm glad I spoke to you about this" And lifting a five pound lump hammer he advanced on the machine with the clear intention of smashing it in smithereens.

"No, no, no Professor I can't let you do this" I reached out to catch his wrist and pull the hammer out of his grasp "Think of all the good you could do with it, you could end world hunger and bring about universal peace to name but a few"

As the argument raged between us, I became convinced that I would not be able to prevail against his rooted objections, so I did the only sensible thing. I clocked him with the hammer, stole the machine and that's how I became the supreme ruler of the world.

Property of the State

He was no ordinary hero, If the truth must be told, he was an arrant coward. He had a mile wide yellow streak running from the crown of his head, splitting at his arse and continuing down each leg to the base of his heels.

He wasn't at all put out by his cowardice, however. He lived mostly by the old Slattery, of mounted fut fame, family motto, better a coward for five minutes than a dead man all your life.

The premium placed by society on bravery and heroism was a source of considerable puzzlement to him and newspaper accounts of brave deeds by folk who dived into torrential rivers to rescue half drowned kittens gave him, not to put a tooth in it, a severe case of the pip.

One thing did, somewhat, get his dander up. Whenever he came across a notice, be it on a hoarding or some of the multitudinous grand buildings one comes across in ones perambulations around the town, saying Property of the State - Keep out. This otherwise innocuous warning seemed to him to represent the elevation of the state over the rights and entitlements of the general populace.

After all, when all is said and done, what is the State if not the agglomeration of all its citizens?

So, who then has the right, in our friend's mind, to deny him, and all the rest of the multitude, entry to these many and various properties?

This resentment came to a head over a comparatively minor altercation between himself and a large specimen of the Garda Siochana on North Earl Street one Easter Monday when, finding his passage blocked off from O'Connell Street owing access to the parade being reserved, not for the heroes of the Easter Rising, since they were all long gone to their celestial reward, but for their descendants, even unto the third and fourth generation.

As person of advanced years, and a citizen of the state for all of those years, he felt that he should be entitled to proceed by the shortest route to his destination, in his case Anne's Cafe on Henry Street, a favourite breakfast spot of his, but this obdurate member of the constabulary stood four square in his path.

After a brief, I will, you won't, conversation he was overcome by a momentary rush of blood to his head.

He snatched the copper's hat off his ginger head, tossed it under a passing bread van, shouted "Tochaigh Ar La" and shambled away as fast as he could.

Sadly, for him, the policeman was swifter than one might expect, given his extraordinary girth and our hero was confined in durance vile for three months for conduct likely to lead to a breach of the peace.

Needless to state, this being Ireland, he only served three days, after which he was unceremoniously thrust back into the general population.

Confounded Ambition

Prince Rupert was very put out. Just to clarify, Rupert was a cock Turkey and an exceedingly proud one at that. However, he had had a disturbing experience earlier in the day and was now stomping around the lower well field muttering and squawking under his breath.

"What's got your tail feathers in a twist?" Demanded Bernard the bull. He was called Bernard because he was a pure bred Limousin bull, not, you will understand a native of France himself, but both his mother and father were native to that fair land and consequently he gloried in the name Bernard.

"Look at me" Snarled Rupert "Am I not the most exquisite example of the avian species ever seen in this, or any other part of the World?"

"Well to tell the truth Rupe, you do look quite fine with that dramatic spread of tail feathers and your assured mien when perambulating around the farmstead. But what has that got to do with anything?" Asked Bernard.

"That impertinent little sparrow has had the temerity to suggest that because I don't fly, I'm somehow less of a bird than he is because he does. It's deeply insulting I tell you" he was, as has been pointed out earlier, very put out "And don't call me Rupe, It's Prince Rupert, if you don't mind.

"You can fly, you know" Said Bernard

"What do you mean I can fly? Demanded Rupert "I should know if I can fly or not, and I most certainly cannot fly. Please don't be unnecessarily nasty to me, you're worse than the bloody sparrow"

"I may have misspoken myself" Replied Bernard in a lofty tone of voice "What I mean is that I can help you to fly, it's surprisingly easy, really"

"You teach me to fly, don't be ridiculous, you're a great lumbering bovine, how could you teach me to fly, it's patently impossible"

"Listen you obnoxious prat" Snapped Bernard "I said help you, not teach you. All you have to do is eat a half dozen of those brown cake like things you can find lying around the paddock"

"You're telling me that in order to be able to fly, all I have to do is eat a half dozen of your shits. That's disgusting. You must take me for a complete fool"

"In all of our acquaintance" said Bernard " Have you ever known me to tell anything but the plain unvarnished truth. You can do what you like, of course, but if you want to put the upstart sparrow in his place, all you need to do is exactly as I've told you. After all, how do you think he's able to fly?"

With considerable trepidation Rupert decided that he'd give it a try. Imagine his amazement when after consuming his sixth cowpat he felt an enormous lightness throughout his body and with a tremendous leap he soared into the clear blue sky.

Sometime later after lapping the field several times he came to rest on the topmost branch of the grand old cedar tree in the corner.

As he was squeaking his triumph to the whole world the farmer arrived and spotting Rupert on his high point, he whipped up his shotgun and with one well aimed shot brought the poor foolish bird to the ground.

Reynard the fox was lurking in the undergrowth and turning to his little Cubs playing round his tail he said "You can always rely on bullshit to get you to the top, but it won't keep you there

Crushed

"Bye gorgeous', she said. 'I'll see you in another ten years' time" and turning athletically she strode up the granite steps of number 5 Cavendish Row.

Glenn gazed distractedly at her retreating form as she disappeared into the gallery, wondering just what he had said to cause this cavalier treatment.

"I thought we had a good thing going here" he called out, but too late as the big Georgian door slammed shut with a resounding boom.

"Bloody women!" he snarled and headed off to the warm embrace of his favourite boozer.

The following morning, early afternoon really, he woke with a pounding headache and a blinding winter sunlight blasting directly into his eyes through a crack in the hastily drawn curtains. Swearing lustily, he staggered into the kitchen hoping that there was some coffee left from last night. His brother was cheerfully whistling and buttering toast at the kitchen table and he greeted Glenn with entirely inappropriate cheerfulness.

"Hey Bro" he cried, "How did it go last night, did she swoon and say yes?"

"Will you for God's sake tone it down, stop the whistling and bread scraping. Can't a man have a little peace and quiet in the morning?" Pleaded Glenn

"Oh dear, things didn't go well last night I guess" Peter commiserated "What happened, it's just a small glitch I imagine"

"You could say that" moaned Glenn "She told me she'd see me in ten years' time. I figure that means that she's broken it off, wouldn't you say?'

"Remember what Ma used to say, Sharper than a serpent's tooth is the tongue of an ungrateful woman. I reckon when she come to her senses, she'll be back on her bended knees begging for forgiveness" Peter tended towards unrealistic optimism.

"I remember she also used to say - never run after a woman or a bus, there'll be another one along in a minute" Glen muttered "I'm going out for a drink, how about you?"

Literati

They woke up to the woods deep in two feet of snow and Oscar declaimed "To live is the rarest thing in the world, most people exist, that's all"

"Oh, for God's sake Oscar, would you ever stop with the witty aphorisms" Shaw snapped "Here we are with snow up to our oxters and all you can do is trot out one of your famous witticisms. You make me tired sometimes"

Oscar retired in a thunderous sulk into the shadows near the stairs "some people don't know when they're in the presence of genius" he grumbled and tossed down a large slug of fifteen year old whiskey from his chased silver hip flask.

Joyce peered out the window through his bottle bottom glasses and vainly rubbed the glass to clear the condensation "I'm inclined to the idea" he said "That this writers retreat may not have been the brightest notion. It was bad enough to that we chose the depths of winter, but Oregon in December? We really should have thought this thing through. Mind you GB, I do think you're a little bit hard on Oscar, he's only a young fella and he's probably missing smart society in London. This isn't exactly his thing now is it?"

Suddenly he removed his glasses and rubbed them on his tie "Either my eyes are even worse than I thought or there's someone out there on the beach, looks like they're going in for a dip"

The others crowded around him, straining to see who might be deranged enough to be swimming off an Oregon beach in two feet of snow.

"Godammit" snarled Oscar "It's that little toad Lord Alfred Douglas. I warned him that if he came within 500 yards of me, I'd drag his skinny arse out for a duel. Where's my overcoat, I'll kill the little shit"

"I can't allow that sort of carry on in my company" Said Shaw "If there's one thing I stand for its pacifism. I'm totally opposed to all forms of violence and I just won't stand for it"

Joyce and Gogarty meanwhile were physically restraining Oscar. "Settle down man" said Gogarty "The Ballad of Reading Gaol may have been a great work of art but if you kill a member of the nobility it's something more permanent that a spell in jug. Leave it go, he's not worth your life Oscar"

"Oh bollix" Oscar said despondently "Experience is simply the name we give to our mistakes" and he turned for consolation to his hip flask.

Opposition

Danny was a bit pissed off with his esteemed friends and colleagues in the writers group. He'd spent laborious hours setting up an excursion to the rain forest in South America, plane fares, accommodation, in tents, of course, food, campfire cooking, of course and all ancillary services.

But did his efforts receive the kind of rapturous appreciation he'd expected? Did they my arse?

First up to challenge him was Felicity, well known for her negative response to all efforts and none "What about the Ku Klux Klan" she demanded.

"The Ku Klux Klan?" Danny asked, deeply puzzled "What's the Ku Klux Klan got to do with anything, we're talking about South America here, as far as I know they only infest the United States, they'd hardly be welcome in the rain forests, most of the residents down there are persons of a very different ethnic origin than your average red neck yank. Besides the head buck cat of the red necks is Donald Trump himself and he, famously, doesn't much like people from south of the border, so the Ku Klux Klan is the least of our worries"

"So" Josephine piped up from the fourpenny seats "What about the sanitary facilities, I've heard that the rain forest is home to all manner of creepy crawlys. I don't fancy going behind a bush only to meet up with a hungry anaconda"

"Ah, get a grip" cried Jimmy, tired an emotional as usual as off his face with a cocktail of mind altering substances "Who gives a shit about sanitary facilities anyway?"

With a profound sigh of exasperation Danny said "Tell you what, why don't we forget about the rain forest and we'll go to Sligo instead. I'm sick of all the opposition, I've gone right off the whole idea"

Rosinante

"Your invitation is extremely attractive" said Alonso "but unfortunately I have other pressing engagements elsewhere"

As he spoke, he thought "I'm sorry I said that now"

"Are you quite sure" The young girl in the flimsy clothing and the gossamer wings asked, "I had something very special in mind for you this evening?"

"I'm not normally one to look a gift horse in the mouth, in fact, if you ask any of my friends, they'd be astonished that I would turn down an opportunity to spend time with a pretty girl like you. However, I have a long, long way to go before bedtime and I have undertaken some tasks which will demand all my full attention. Perhaps another time?"

From behind his back James horse Rosinante snorted "Jeez Al, never mind all the promises you have to keep and the miles to go before you sleep thing. Even Robert Frost wouldn't miss an opportunity like this and him a poet and all. Just go for it man"

The young girl, Felicity, a nymph of the forest said "You should listen to your long faced friend James. Come with me and you will have a night that even in the thousand and one nights it would be spoken of with bated breath. My Father's palace lies not two leagues distant in the forest and tonight is the Winter Solstice. The longest night of the year. We woodland folk are famous for our parties and this one is likely to go down in history" As she spoke her face lit up with a smile and around her spread an aura of pink glowing light.

With a delightful trill of merriment, she rose up on her wings and commenced a seductive dance around James head "Alonso, Alonso" She whispered "When you are old a grey you will have a tale of wonder to tell the little ones gathered at your knee. The bones of that tale are yours to experience, you can tell them of the evening you met Felicity the forest nymph, heard your trusty steed give you advice and trudged dutifully off to keep the empty promises which had been dragged from you under pressure, or you could regale them with tales of wonder from the Palace Under The Mountain, where the ancient King sits, surrounded by his Elven court.

You could watch their open mouthed amazement as you relate to them the extraordinary music which was played on that night and the unbelievable foods which were prepared for the exalted guests. You may wish to keep the remainder of the night to yourself until they are old enough to appreciate that part of the tale"

Tossing her mane Rosinante galloped off into the enchanted forest shouting back over her shoulder as she went "You can go the miles before you sleep, I'm off to the fairy gig, you're on yer own mate"

Chaos in Government

The note was left in the foyer of Government Buildings, placed within an empty Amazon carton which had originally held a book. It read, in blood coloured ink:

"Enda Kenny has been taken by the Emerald army and will be returned on payment of ten million Euros, to be deposited in the Offshore Bank of Abductors in the Cayman Islands. If the ransom hasn't been paid by Friday next, the price for his return goes up to twenty million Euros. For further information call 0876633890"

Richard Bruton studied the communication with interest "Mmm, I wonder how much they would ask if we told them to keep him?" He mused.

As he sat in splendid isolation, in his ministerial office, contemplating his chances of being elevated to the Taoiseach-hood the door shuddered under a thunderous knocking.

"Come on in, for God's sake, before you take the door off i's hinges" Richard snarled.

The door was thrust open and banged off the filing cabinet directly behind it, revealing the twin substantial, figures of Phil Hogan and James Reilly

"What's this I hear about our Glorious Leader being snatched, can it be true, Achone, agus achone. How are we supposed to function without his tender hand on the tiller of state?" Queried big Phil

Reilly, never one to be outdone in his choice of hyperbole, cried "Richard, for The sake of the Party, what are we going to do, and the troika, will somebody think of the troika. There'll be panic in the markets and a run on the banks. We'll be moidered entirely, so we will. You have to do something, Richard, otherwise all is lost" and he wiped a tear from the corner of his eye.

"Now lads" Richard said in his best, pouring oil on troubled waters voice "Hold on a minute here, it's not all bad, we all know that he's been slipping badly in the polls lately and the Irish people are suckers for a hard luck story. This could be the very bump we need in the popularity stakes. Irish Water, McNulty, Expenses and Allowances, they'll all be gone off the headlines. We'll be the most popular party once again. In fact, I've just been thinking, it's only an idea mind, but, now hear me out, we could spring a snap election, you know, appeal to the patriotism of the people. It might just work, you know"

"But Enda" Whined Big Phil "What about Enda?"

"We'll give him a state funeral" Replied Richard "The Irish people like nothing better than a spectacle, we could have a hearse drawn by six black horses with plumes and everything.

We'd need a new Taoiseach, of course, if you guys will put my name forward, I'll see you right after I'm elected. You can count on me"

After the other two had left, Richard opened the cabinet behind his desk and said to the crouching Enda squashed, bound and gagged inside "Hard luck Enda, You're surplus to requirement now"

Martian Volleyball

"Oh God, I've married a Martian"

"Martians, as everyone knows are dark brown in colour, tiny in stature and travel around in huge, hulking walking machines, due to the fact that Mars gravity is so much less than ours. If you don't believe me, look up Orson Welles and War of the Worlds, that'll explain everything you need to know. Given the undoubted veracity of the foregoing I fail to see how you could be amazed/upset at being married to one"

"That's easy for you to say, you weren't dazzled by his stunning brown skin, immense walking machine and unimaginable world knowledgeableness. We met just after London and New York had been destroyed and he had taken a break from havoc wreaking and general depredation to travel around and see the scenery. He especially liked the cliffs of Moher. He said they reminded him of his original nesting place on the slopes of Mount Olympus, that's on Mars you know"

My mother didn't like him from the start, especially when he started to eat her, starting from the feet up. You may not know this, but Martians are foot fetishists, almost to a Martian. Anyway, mama's objections were soon a moot point, since he quickly reached her mouth and after that she had nothing of importance to say for herself, or anyone else either.

Dad, on the other hand thought he'd make a great match for me, especially after he'd eaten mother. He said that anyone with a cast iron digestion like that couldn't be all bad. Besides, he told me that travel broadens the mind and that surely as soon as they had destroyed the earth and all the people on it, they would very likely set off around the Galaxy, plundering and looting wherever their fancy took them. Dad was a bit dubious about what's his names mother. Mothers in law can be a bit of a trial after all and add in the racial mixture issue and things could get a bit sticky but Whatsit reassured him on that score by explaining that on the marriage night it was customary for the bride and groom to ceremonially eat the Mother in Law, starting from the feet up"

"So, what's with the surprise/shock at the discovery that's you married one?"

"Well, what he didn't tell me was that you can't play volleyball on Mars because the gravity is so weak that if you bounced a volleyball, even a soft one it'd take off into space and never be seen again. The expense of volleyball season would be prohibitive. If I'd known that beforehand it would have been a deal breaker"

Mother Love

Annie had mistakenly wandered onto the nudist beach in Sandycove and couldn't find her way back. "Ah the devil pickle it" she said, shucking her clothes "Hitler took a chance and look where he finished up"

Lying spread eagled in the blazing sunshine on a secluded part of the beach she concluded that all this fuss about nudism was not really necessary.

Suddenly she heard the unmistakable sound of her mother's dulcet tones offering her hidebound opinions in a loud and disapproving voice. "Marjorie" she said, in stentorian tones, addressing her long suffering companion. "This carry on is utterly disgraceful. If God had meant us to gad about naked, he'd never have provided us with clothes. It's unnatural, so it is. There really ought to be a law against it"

Marjorie, a timid and unprepossessing lady of uncertain years said "Oh Jane, I always thought that our ancestors, you know, Adam and Eve, were starkers in the garden of Eden. So, if it was alright for them maybe it's ok for these people. You remember when we went to that church in Torrevieja on the Costa Brava last year, there were nudists on the beach there and no one seemed to take any notice"

"Good old Marjorie" murmured Annie as she frantically struggled to scramble into her clothes, hopefully without drawing the attention of her harridan mother. "With any luck she'll draw down the wrath of God on her head, together with a lecture on the failure of moral turpitude in the modern youth and give me time to sneak away undiscovered"

Sadly, for Annie her cunning plan was doomed to failure. As she scrambled into her knickers her mother's eagle eye fell on her and with a wrathful howl she strode over to her errant daughter. "What's the meaning of this disgraceful behaviour?" Demanded the irate parent "I didn't raise my daughter to display all her parts for the delectation of the multitude on this rocky beach. What would your sainted father think if he could see you now"

"Mother" Annie said, deciding that a strong defence was better than an abject retreat "There's nothing wrong with the human body, it was given to us by God and after all, we've all seen everything before. You should try it out yourself"

"Ah the devil pickle it" said the Mother, shucking her clothes "Hitler took a chance, and look where he finished up"

Championship Ambitions

"She'll be a world champion someday" said her Dad proudly.

"OK" Replied her frosty faced Aunt Jane "But a world champion what. She's nothing much to look at, she has two left feet, she's not very bright and, let's face it, in the get up and go department she has got up and went already"

Jane's sister, the putative champion's Mum looked very upset at this, somewhat harsh, criticism of her one and only duckling.

"That's not a nice way to be talking about your niece, Jane" she quavered timorously "She's a good girl, always ready to help around the house. Admittedly she's broken more China than the Boxer rebellion, and she did suck the cats tail up in the Hoover, but that was just the once."

"And what about her little adventure with the goldfish" Demanded Jane, now well up on her high horse, she wasn't used to being confronted, especially by her younger sister "We all know about that fiasco, don't we?"

"Now that's just not fair Jane. You know as well as everyone else that she felt sorry for the poor fish and wanted to make him dry and warm. How was she supposed to know that's fishes don't live out of water, particularly when wrapped in fluffy towels?"

The proud Dad who had been fulminating silently in the corner during this exchange burst into incandescence. "That's enough from you two. Jane, if you can't say a good word, say nothing. I will not have anyone casting nasturtiums on my little treasure. She's just getting through a growth spurt. When she grows into herself, she'll be a world beater, you mark my words"

Jane rose to her full five feet in height and with an imperious scowl she snarled "Grows into herself indeed. The girl is forty five years old, she's never had a job in her life, she has no marriage prospects and she's penniless. You two need to wake up and smell the coffee" And turning she attempted to make a grand exit.

As she reached out to the door handle the door crashed inwards hitting her smack in the face and knocking her sprawling across the room. The subject of the conversation dashed into the room holding what appeared to be as dead rat at arm's length. "Daddy, Daddy" She wailed "The Ferret is dead, I left him in the freezer because I thought he was too hot in his fur coat, but I forgot about him and now he's dead"

Vain Attempt

"I'm trying, I'm trying" he said

"You've been trying my patience for the last fifty two years" she snapped "You don't have to tell me you're trying"

"That wasn't what I meant, and you know it very well. It's not very nice to take advantage of someone whose as imbrangled as me you know. If you were in my shoes you wouldn't be half as cranky as you are"

"Imbrangled is it? Is that even a word? I think you just made it up"

"There you go again, if James Joyce could invent a whole new language why can't I make up a measly word? anyway I'm sure I heard someone on the radio using that word last week" he ventured, scratching his aged head.

"Look it up on Google, if it's not on Google it doesn't exist" She crowed triumphantly.

"Google me arse" his temper exhausted he turned on her "It's all google and the Internet and social media these days. When we were young there was none of that nonsense and we were no worse off without it. That bloody iPhone has driven you out of your mind. Every time I look at you, your face is stuck in it, checking your what's app or face time or some other bloody thing. It's enough to drive a body to drink, so it is"

"I'm going into town" she announced "There's a protest on at the GPO. It's about the abuse of the tax system by foreign companies, or was it equality for the downtrodden? Hang on a minute and I'll look it up"

With a profound sigh of exasperation, he grabbed his cap and headed out the door, calling over his shoulder as he went "Im off to the pub, don't say I didn't warn you. You've driven me to the demon drink"

As the door slammed behind him, with head bowed and thumbs flickering over the keys of the iPhone she asked "What's that you say? Just let me get this latest text from my sister and you can bring me up to date on what you were trying to do"

Dubious Alliances

"Renfrew, would you be good enough to repeat what you told me for The Minister for Extrasolar affairs. To be entirely honest I find the whole story quite impossible to believe" the speaker of the house of exemplary artificers on planet XY looked somewhat shocked as he spoke

Renfrew, not used to the stratospheric heights of ministerial office stammered as he began "It's like this, your worshipfulness. I was sent by my employers to suss out trade prospects in the outer arm of the Milky Way Galaxy and what I found there beggars belief. I can't blame Mr Speaker for finding it hard to believe. Even I, and I was there, find it hard to credit some of the things I saw on the planet the inhabitants call Earth, the one that orbits their sun which is called Sol"

"The planet is stunningly beautiful with about three fifths of its surface covered by oceans and the other two fifths has some of the most astonishingly fabulous landscapes in the known universe.

Sadly, the people on the planet appear to have no appreciation of the wonders of their planet. About half of them are located in what is sometimes termed The Western world or, often the First World. The others inhabit the third world. As far as I could see, there was no second world, however the unfortunate dwellers in the third world live, for the most part, in abject poverty, despite being surrounded with a natural abundance of the necessities of life. These are owned and controlled by a favoured few, often denizens of the western nations. These few are determined to hold onto their, often ill gotten, gains despite the glaringly self evident needs of the majority.

"More shocking than that, if that were possible is their penchant for warfare. At any one time the planet is wracked by dozens of conflicts, otherwise known as Wars, Revolutions, Coups or Tribal disagreements. All off these conflicts have one thing in common, they involve massive deaths, mainly in the most horrific ways. By far and away the vast majority of these deaths are inflicted on innocent bystanders who have, to use an Earth phrase 'No Dog in the Fight' that, unfortunately does not protect them from the bombs and bullets of the combatants"

"Speaking from an outsiders' perspective, the population in general seems to have a death wish, pursuing, as they do, many inherently dangerous practices. They overeat, causing potentially fatal illness, smoke tobacco which destroys their lungs, drink excessive amounts of alcohol which befuddles their senses and rots their livers."

"All things considered; we'd be well advised to steer well clear of them. They are toxic"

Topsy Turvey House

Freddie looked out the window in open mouthed amazement "Everything's upside down outside" he said to his immediate superior who was calmly knitting in her favourite armchair.

"Don't be silly dear" she replied "It's this house"

"What's this house?" Freddie demanded "Why can't you ever make an observation without obscuring it in gnomic folderol?'

"It's this house that's upside down, you fool, not the entire world outside" and she calmly continued knitting, muttering to herself in a sing song voice "Knit one, purl one, cast one off"

"Now who's the fool. How could the house be upside down, we'd be sitting on the ceiling if that was the case? Since we're not sitting on the ceiling, the house is not upside down, ipso facto" Freddie was particularly pleased with this sally, he didn't often get one over on his beloved spouse but in this case, he definitely felt that he had outsmarted her.

Laying her knitting down with an exasperated sigh she said "You never listen to a word I say. I told you last night before we went to bed that I had made a deal with the good fairy in the forest to set the house to rights. I'm sick to death with all the housework I'm stuck with and I thought she'd be able to wave a magic wand and sort it out for me. Somehow my request got mixed up in translation from English to elvish and now we find ourselves inverted, house, people, untidiness and all"

"A fairy you say?" Queried Freddie "I have no recollection of this alleged conversation, are you sure it's not some cockamamie story you've cooked for your writing group? Anyway, since you're accepting responsibility for this brouhaha, I assume you have something in hand to put everything to rights. I need to go to work and I can hardly do it standing on my head, so chop, chop, let's get it sorted"

"It's not so simple" the light of his life replied "We need to propitiate the fairies somehow, you know, with an offering like. they won't accept that it's their cock up, so we have to make nice to them"

"Make nice? Make nice? Are you out of your tiny mind? Between you and your ephemeral buddies in the trees we're stuck in an upside down house and you want me to pay to have it sorted, I'd rather a root canal any day" and he barged out the kitchen door and fell ten feet, to his ultimate demise, on his noggin.

Wish in one Hand

Gina, Mary and Frances met in their favourite watering hole to discuss their upcoming holidays.

"Well guys" says Mary, the most outspoken of the three "What's the story? I've got a great deal for a fourteen day break in the Virgin Islands, it'll only cost three grand each. What do you think?

Gina looked a bit dubious "I dunno, three grand is a bit out of my holiday budget, it sounds delightful but I'm not sure what him indoors would think"

Frances, ever the problem solver, interjected "No worries, me and Mary will give a dig out for the balance. It's a once in a lifetime experience"

After some negotiations and arm twisting, Gina reluctantly agreed, worrying about what her devoted spouse would make of him being left with the ankle biters for two weeks unsupervised. to her considerable he enthusiastically agreed. "it's a great idea pet" he said, "and don't worry about the cost, I've a little bit put away for a rainy day. or in this instance a sunny fortnight"

Everything went swimmingly until they went out on whale watching tour in the Caribbean. The drunken boat captain ran the boat aground and fell overboard, drowning before the girls had an opportunity to break his neck.

Checking out their surroundings the girls were devastated to find themselves cast a shore on a desert island.

"what do we do now?" demanded Gina

"We'll just have to suck it up" Said Mary, jumping into problem solver mode "We'll be back home in no time"

Sadly, she was being overly optimistic. Three years passed and the girls were still marooned when a bottle floated up on the beach.

France's rushed to pick the bottle up and wrenched it open. As soon as she popped the cork a wisp of blue smoke floated and enlarged into a genie.

"I've been in that blasted bottle for a thousand years so I'm going to give you all a wish each.

France's rushed in first "I'm sick and tired living on fish every day, I'd like to be sat in the saddle room in. The Shelbourne with a massive fillet steak in front of me.

"No problem" he said and with poof she disappeared.

Gina came next, "I hate sleeping in the bloody sand with creepy crawlies all over me, I wish I was at home in my own bed"

"Consider it done" He said, and she was gone too.

Mary looked around with forlorn look and said "It's lonely here without the girls, I wish they were back"

Control Issues

Thomas the tank engine huffed and puffed his way into the terminus. Heaving a sigh of contentment, he said to the Fat Controller "Thank god that day is over, I thought it'd never end"

The fat controller, however had other ideas. "Sorry Thomas, but Percy has managed to become derailed again and as you're the only engine available you'll just have to go out and rescue him"

"Oh, to hell with it" Snarled Thomas "Why can't Gordon do it. After all he's the "Big engine" isn't he? Anyway, what is it with that dozey cretin Percy? Seems that lately every time he goes out on a run, he either crashes into the buffers at the end or he runs off the stupid track. Never mind, I'm going home, let him sort himself out. I've just about had it with the lot of ye"

Flushed in the face and almost speechless the Fat Controller tried to tone down Thomas's language down "Now, now" he said soothingly "Let's not lose our cool here Thomas. This is, after all, a children's programme. That sort of language should be kept for the marshalling yards. What's got into you Thomas? This sort of response is not at all what we expect from you. Kindly moderate your behaviour or I'll be forced to leave you out of the next five episodes"

"Janey Mack and whatsisface, please do. This series is getting on my wow. I'll have you know that I've had offers from the Orient Express and the Trans Canada Pacific Railroads to come work for them. The only thing that keeps me on this crap show is that Emily keeps giving me the glad eye. I know she's a

198

bit out of my class but hope springs eternal, know what I mean?"

"Dear God" muttered the fat controller "He's obviously lost his marbles" and he hurriedly made chopping motions for the cameraman to cut shooting.

So concentrated was he on his signals that he didn't notice that he had stepped backwards onto the track. He stumbled and fell prone across both tracks and struggled in vain to get up as his girth made him easier to go over than to circumvent.

Seeing him helpless in front of him Thomas gave a great snort and lunged forward, neatly dividing the unfortunate controller into three unequal pieces.

"Do I feel embarrassed?" He queried "Do I hell"

Christmas Cheer

"What do ya mean, he has several aliases?" snapped Sergeant O'Leary. He was feeling more than usually fed up with life, the world and things in general. It was the dark, dank, foggy and gloomy month of January, his dog had died by choking on a turkey drumstick on Christmas Day and his wife had run off with the milkman on St Stephens day and to make his suffering even more excruciating he had looked upon the wine whilst it was red the night before to a most unwise degree.

Now to put the proverbial tin hat on it this over ambitious and exceedingly pompous young Garda, fresh out of Templemore had dragged this unfortunate left over from the Christmas season in and wanted to charge him with vagrancy, begging and being without visible means of support.

"Now sarge, there's no point in shooting the messenger here. The man, if man he actually is, was apprehended in Grafton Street, soliciting alms from the ordinary people going about their lawful occasions. When I confronted him and asked if he could identify himself, he replied, in a slurred and somewhat incomprehensible fashion, that if I could supply the mirror then he could identify himself quite readily.

I immediately upbraided him for his attitude and warned him of the dreadful consequences of obstructed the Gardai in the pursuit of their duties.

Adopting a considerably improved manner he then reeled off several alleged names under which he asked me to believe that he customarily referred to himself. He further assured me that he was a well known figure in the neighbourhood and that all I would need to do, to allay any misgivings I might have about his credentials, was to ask anybody who he was.

Furthering my enquiries, I demanded his address and he immediately informed me that his normal abode was The North Pole. Finding this information unlikely in the extreme, I then demanded his citizenship papers or his work permit which would entitle him to be resident in the state, or in the absence of such ID documents his airline ticket to return him to his residence. He replied that he did not carry such documentation about his person as he normally had his pockets so stuffed with presents for small children that there was no room for extraneous paperwork. Furthermore, he informed me that he was allergic to airline travel and that his preferred mode of transport was a sleigh drawn by nine reindeer. Upon enquiring as to the whereabouts of the said sleigh he entered into a long and rambling tale of excess alcohol, lack of snow and something about a Bolshie employee named Rudolf. At that point I cautioned him and brought him to the station"

"Well" snarled the irate sergeant "Guess what you'll be getting in your stocking next year"

Fireman Sam

"Hey guys, good to meet youse, I don't think I've met any of you before" said fireman Sam in his usual, somewhat annoying manner "I'm fireman Sam" he continued "maybe you guys would like to introduce yourselves"

"You can't be fireman Sam" snapped the one nearest to him "I'm Fireman Sam"

Hardly had he spoken than a clamour broke out amongst all four of them, each one claiming prior ownership of the Fireman Sam title.

"This is bloody silly" Complained the first Sam "Some fool in continuity must have gotten something mixed up. As anyone who knows anything knows I'm the one and only Fireman Sam, these other guys are either clones or imposters or both. I'm getting on to the director to get this mess sorted out"

One of the others, it was difficult to sort out exactly which, as none of them were comfortable with either numbers or letters attached to them as there would then be an obvious pecking order to their existence and who wants to be paddy last I the line, anyway, one of the others, obviously of a more contemplative bent than the others said "You know, even if you are convinced that you are the real deal here, that's no

202

guarantee that you're right. After all, if we are, indeed, identical, then we must all have the identical set of memories, genes etc. So, we may be utterly indistinguishable one from another"

"Well bollix to that" asserted the one who might or might not have been the first speaker "I'm a unique and distinct, standalone person in my own right. I refuse to acknowledge that anyone else is indistinguishable from me. I've said it before, and I'll say it again I'M THE ONE AND ONLY FIREMAN SAM. All the rest of you are obviously rejects from some counterfeiting operation. So why don't you all go to the recycling centre and get yourselves melted down. Who knows, next time you might become one of the characters from Frozen, you never know your luck"

The other three, casting a conspiratorial glance amongst themselves grabbed hold of the speaker and threw him headfirst into the house fire which had been raging merrily whilst they debated life, the universe and everything.

None of them noticed the man leaving the premises with the six hotdogs which he'd brought to the house party next door.

Wedding Cake

I mean! Walking off the bloody wedding cake, and on my first day in my first job. What the hell got into her; it can't have been anything I said. I never got a chance to open my gob.

I'm standing there, one arm as long as the other, dressed up like a bleeding penguin when without a word she ups and storms off. I sincerely hope that I get paid for this gig, after all it's not my fault that she's pulled a Sinead O'Connor.

Oh Janey Mack, here's the director. "What's that you say? Just carry on as if nothing has happened?" Now that doesn't make any sense. The fundamental thing about a wedding cake is that it needs a bride and a groom. Without the bride it's about a useful as an ice pick in the Sahara Desert. Still he's paying the piper so I might as well give him his money's worth.

"How's this" I ask, posing as if she were still there with a saccharine smile showing my pearly whites to best effect. Trained in the Stanislavski acting school and using his celebrated Method Acting technique I had no trouble in visualising her in all her virginal glory and I gave it the best shot that I was capable of.

Posturing and posing I soon got right into the bones of my role as groom to the absent bride. The rest of the team continued as though oblivious to the absence of what might be argued as the star of the show, obviously they were all familiar with Stanislavski's method as I was.

The director shouted through his megaphone, the cameraman cranked his camera, the best boy did whatever it is the best boy does and the grip, who carries the keys around, carried the keys around.

Finally, at the end of the afternoon the director called out, "right, cut and print. That's a wrap" sorely puzzled but satisfied that I had earned my first pay cheque I made my way home. My mother was waiting with a lovely meal prepared and a host of questions as to how the day had gone.

"Difficult to say, mother, you'd have to have been there" I replied tiredly. "I guess you could call it show business"

Rockfall

The coast road was blocked by falling rocks leaving poor Francesca distraught because she had left the baby in his cot while she nipped out for a bottle of Prosecco.

"This looks like a job for Superman" said the man of steel who happened to be loitering nearby in a now rare and unusual phone box.

Bursting forth from his confinement and tearing the door off its hinges in the process he flew at several times the speed of sound to Francesca's aid. The fact that she was a stunning blonde bombshell was entirely secondary consideration for our hero, he was, after all, continually surrounded by damsels in distress, each one of them more pulchritudinous than the last and even heavenly beauty is bound to pall with constant repetition.

"What kept you?" Demanded Francesca as she took another slug from her severely depleted bottle of supermarket plonk "There's a baby in trouble you know" she slurred "We're conditioned to expect an instant response from our Superheroes, I'm afraid I'll have to report you to the Justice League of America. This kind of tardiness is just not acceptable"

Swooping down he snatched her up in his arms and headed off in the direction of her now squalling offspring. Only Superman could hear the child's pathetic whimpering as he was some distance from the rockfall and they could not travel at supersonic speeds as Francesca's clothes would be torn from her body by the fierce rush of wind and he is, as everybody knows, the essence of gentlemanliness.

As they flew on their merry way, he upbraided her on her very obvious neglect of the unfortunate infant "How could you leave an infant all alone while you went out to buy booze?" He demanded "I should really be reporting you to child services for neglect"

"Are you serious?" snarled Francesca "I needed a bracer and the little git is too small to send to the shops, one of us had to do it, didn't we?"

Tiger in a Bubble

"Ma" cried Jason "There's a tiger in my bubble"

"Yes dear" replied his mother, anxious not to be disturbed as she worked on her magnum opus, which was going to make her famous, sell in uncountable numbers, be translated into 47 languages and be snapped up by a Hollywood mogul for multiple millions.

"No Ma" Jason shouted "I mean it. There's a tiger in my bubble, at least, to be entirely specific there's a tiger's head in my bubble" He was a precocious little git at the best of times, which this was not.

"Jason, what have we told you about using your outdoor voice indoors? Employing your creativity is all well and good but Mummy is busy just now. I'll talk to you in half an hour when I've finished this chapter, meantime you continue playing with your bubbles"

As she delved deeper into her story, she failed to notice the screams and feral growls echoing from the playroom until suddenly a deafening silence descended on the household. Her own mother had often told her that it's when they're quiet that they're at their most destructive. Sighing theatrically, she got up from her desk and made her way into the playroom.

Entering Jason's sanctum, she was amazed to be confronted by a full grown Bengal Tiger lying on the rug in a somnambulant coma with a severely distended stomach and no sign of her one and only.

"Oh Jason" she murmured "What have you done?" and she turned and exited the room, locking the door behind her. Slumped on the bottom step of the stairs she called the emergency services.

Her call was quickly answered "Emergency Services here, which service do you require? police, fire or ambulance?"

"I'm not entirely sure" She replied "It's my son, Jason, you see. He's been eaten by a tiger"

"Madam" said the voice on the other end "It's a very serious offence to make fake calls to the Emergency Services. Large fines can be levied and even prison sentences in particularly bad cases"

Just then Jason's voice impinged on her "Ma, have you met Rajah, my pet tiger. He's just finished the Christmas ham and he's having a nap while I went to the loo. He's pretty cool, isn't he?"

Seen and Not Heard

Mrs Johnson inched towards me clutching her walker, the leash in one hand. The little 'rat on a string' she called a dog, snarled.

"If I were you" Whined Snuffles, for Snuffles was indeed the name of the aforesaid 'rat on a string' "I'd move outta he way and that smartish, she's wicked old besom at the best of times but someone took the milk out of her morning Ovaltine today"

I stood in open mouthed amazement at what was, to all appearances, a talking dog. And not only that but a talking dog who had the temerity to bad mouth Mrs Johnson in front of her face. I had known the old besom for a number of years and considered myself fortunate that I had not met her for a considerable period of time. It seems that she had gone deaf in the interim period, so perhaps the 'rat' wasn't as brave as he seemed.

Suddenly I reeled under the force of a tremendous blow on the back of my head from a walking stick which in my distraction I had failed to notice clutched in Mrs's Johnson's leash free other hand.

"Move over you pillock and don't stand there with your mouth open. Something might fly into it and give you a fit of the heebie jeebies" Snapped the old dear in a saccharine sweet voice completely in contrast to the actual words uttered.

From somewhere in the vicinity of my ankles a voice which was becoming all too familiar piped up "I told you so" Said Snuffles "She gets very aggressive when someone takes the milk outta her Ovaltine at any time of the day, but if it's done first thing in the morning, well, even Genghis Khan would be well advised to steer clear of the old bat"

"Pardon me, Mrs Johnson" I said, timorously, "Do you know that your dog just spoke to me?"

"Speak up" Snapped the old beldam "Civility cost's nothing and it's nice to speak in a clear and concise way when addressing your elders and betters. When I was a young girl, ankle biters like you would be seen and not heard unless spoken to In the first place. There's no common courtesy in the world these days. It's going to hell in a handbasket, so it is"

And raising her stick threateningly, she shuffled out of the room and into the night.

Scaredy Monster

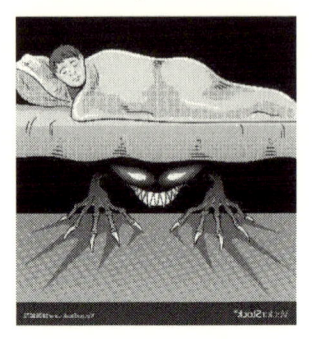

"What the hell ails you, Ugg? you're as twitchy as a cat on a hot tin roof" Flugg asked in his usual concerned fashion, he just couldn't help poking his inverted snout into other people's business.

"It's this red haired kid who sleeps on top of my bed" Ugg moaned "She cries all night and invariably pisses the bed at some point every night. It's above and beyond what any self respecting   Monster should be asked to endure. It's too much" and he thrust his deformed head under his oxter.

"A red haired Kid? You can't be serious, a big fully paid up member of the Monsters Collective can't be bothered by a red haired kid. We in the collective would be forced to take notice if this was to be brought up before the ways and means committee" Flugg didn't look too put out at the prospect of his friends distressing situation nor, to be frank at the prospect of his looming disgrace at the committee hearing.

"For the love of Knugg, don't talk about the ways and means committee. And don't even think of mentioning my embarrassing confession just now. Just put it out of your mind. I'm sorry I even brought it up, though now I think back on it, it was you brought it up" Ugg flushed a vibrant shade of turquoise at this outburst.

"There's a goblin therapist located in Charles Fort, down in Kinsale just outside of Cork city. I could recommend you to him. He's built up a reputation for dealing with issues like yours.

It would be worth the trip to see if he'd be willing to take you on" Flugg was salivating at the prospect of sharing this juicy piece of gossip with his inner circle as soon as Ugg left to go home to his unsavoury bed.

Weeping blood red tears Ugg snivelled "Charles Fort in Cork? How am I supposed to get to Cork? I can hardly rock up to the ticket window in Heuston Station and buy a return ticket on the express.

Anyway I haven't got anything to wear for a meet with a therapist, they like their clients to be dressed smartly, don't they"

"Problems, problems" snapped his friend "For every answer I offer you have another problem, get real can't you. You're a fully fledged Monster aren't you. Just do it"

Back in The Day

Back in the day, when men were men and women were kept in their rightful place, eg, barefoot and pregnant and tied to the kitchen sink, some total gobshite in The Grand Duchy of Finland, then part of the Russian Empire proposed a new law that would give women the vote.

Look at the state of the bloody world now, as a direct consequence of that misguided piece of legislation.

In Germany we have Angela Merkel, a proto-communist whose one aim in life seems to be to do down the unfortunate, hard pressed Irish taxpayer, without the grand duchy gobshite how far up the political tree would Frau Merkel have climbed? Not very I suspect.

Switzerland succumbed to the monstrous regiment of women in 1971 and Lichtenstein in 1984, can it be simple coincidence that they are two of the countries which have remained outside the Euro Zone and that both have the hardest currencies in the world, no, and furthermore I make so bold as to suggest that this blessed state of affairs is due to the foresight and forward thinkingness of the legislators in those countries who barred women, whose brains are obviously not wired for such esoteric pursuits as ruling countries or driving cars, from entering politics until their more astute male relatives had set up a system of, what would be called in Cork, cute hoorism, which has them now firmly ensconced as the worlds, and especially the shady world's bank of last resort.

Leaving this important task in the hands of the fairer sex would have led to catastrophic results. First of all, as soon as they got their hands on the filthy lucre the very first thing they would have done would be to go off and buy shoes, probably in Brown Thomas or some other wildly expensive shoe retailer.

Next stop on the squander path would undoubtedly be a law which compelled all and sundry to go out and equip themselves with knitting needles and skeins of wool which would need the outstretched arms of their downtrodden menfolk being dragooned into service so that the skeins could be wound into balls.

There is no obvious reason why this needs to be done, presumably it's just as efficient to knit from a skein as it is from a ball. Perhaps it's a subtle method of manipulating the men, after all it's a well known fact the men don't do subtle. Mind you little kittens wouldn't have half as much fun with a skein of wool as they do with a ball of same, though that's hardly reason enough to insist on making a balls of it, still we are talking about women here!

Stop and think!

"You know what?" Paddy was struck by a blinding flash of insight "There's two sentences that would make a great chorus for a song"

"I don't want to cast nasturtiums on your enthusiasm" Said his life long buddy Jamsie "But they don't say anything to me beyond that someone is telling someone else that they're about to die and that it'd be a good idea to reflect on their life before the final gong peals"

"Wellll" Paddy mused "Maybe you're right at that. I mean three square metres wouldn't be much use for anything other than a grave while the stop and think thing could just as easily be one of those drink driving ads on television, not that I watch much television. Just as well really, the whores in Leinster House are working themselves up to slapping a television license on computers and tablets. It seems that you can get tele programmes on them as well as on the goggle box in the corner"

"Bloody hell that can't be right, can it?" demanded Jamsie "I've been watching Netflix for the past couple of years secure in the knowledge that those wasters couldn't get their paws on my money. And now you tell me that they're about to get their snouts into a whole new trough of cash? That's just not fair"

"Whoever told you that life was fair" queried Paddy.

As they were speaking a loud wailing cry echoed through the pub in which they were ensconced. "What's that noise?" Asked Jamsie

"Ah, pay no attention, that's just the banshee, you do know that she follows our family because we're from the Macs and the O's"

"Hey, you" he cried, addressing the air over Jamsie's head "Why don't you piss off and haunt some innocent American tourist, if she went home with a tale like that it would pump up the tourism figures in the coming years. Then the gobshites in the Dail wouldn't be interfering in our enjoyment of license free tele"

And he called to the barman "Same again please and would you turn up the volume on the TV"

217

Sherwood

"May all your tomorrows be sunny" He said as he brandished the headsman's axe.

"It's all very well for you to talk" I replied "This bloody block is surprisingly uncomfortable; do you mind if I stand up and stretch my neck?"

"Do you think this is the Ritz or something? We need to move this along, you're not the only one in the queue you know" He shook the axe in a decidedly menacing fashion.

"Listen" I snapped, ill-temperedly "This is my first time for this gig, you've done it hundreds of times. The very least you could do is to have a bit of patience. Civility, as the woman says, costs nuttin, after all"

"Well la di da" he crowed "I'm very sorry your lordship. Far be it from me to interrupt the even tenor of your final moments on earth. By all means, stand up and stretch your neck, and have a bit of a stroll about, while you're about it why don't you. I can afford a few minutes; my time isn't as precious as all that"

Thanking him profusely I scrambled awkwardly to my feet, it's not easy with your hands tied behind your back and performed a series of Prana Bindu exercises designed to bring stress relief and contentment.

As he gaped in astonishment at my contortions, he, and the other sheriffs' men in the castle yard, failed to notice my merry men sneaking in from the outskirts of Sherwood Forest and quietly surrounding the assembled crowd.

Finishing my exercise regime, I turned to the Sheriff and the other luminaries gathered on the raised dais to witness my discomfiture and called up to them;

"Gentlemen, if you would be good enough to turn slightly and look over your shoulders you will notice that each one of you is the target of either one of my archers or alternatively my expert knife fighters. I would therefore suggest that you instruct this ill mannered oaf to release me from my bonds, deposit your arms and jewellery in a neat heap at my feet, provide suitable horses for me and my men and we'll be on our peaceful way"

"One more thing, if it's not too much trouble, would you please send a serf to Maid Marian and ask her to wait for me to pick her up at the castle gate on my way out. Much obliged"

Christmas Shopping

"When Christmas comes around" I said to the woman sitting beside me on the number 14 bus going towards Artane "Our family always have a big meal about three weeks before hand. We call this the Kris Kringle celebration"

She was almost buried under a small mountain of shopping bags and she spent most of the journey rootling in the vast multitude of pucks and parcels, counting, not altogether under her breath, as she fumbled "There's Jacinta's top that I got in Penneys, and that's George's tablet from Argos, now where did I put wee Johnnie's thing, Ah there it is"

I carried on with my story about our family tradition "After the meal is over, we assign everybody another member of the family and they must buy them a Christmas gift. Ideally, they recipient should not know who has been chosen to provide their particular present but, in practice, long before the big day arrives all and sundry usually have a strong suspicion, if not an absolute certainty as to who will be their benefactor. This has, over the years, led to some hysterically funny and a few not so humorous exchanges. Mind you the huge advantage of this system is that everybody only has to buy one present for the entire family"

I couldn't help but notice that her attention seemed to be somewhat lacking as the journey drew on. In point of fact it began to dawn on me that she was more concerned with the contents of her multitudinous parcels than she was with the jewels of wisdom which I was imparting to her. From my perspective it was eminently clear that, if ever there was a case for instituting the Kris Kringle system anywhere, it was in her house.

"Madame" I queried "Am I boring you? It seems to me that you have overburdened yourself with the whole Christmas thing and that you might be better advised to de clutter your life as I have done. See me now, I have only the one present to buy for the family and when that purchase is made, I am free to go about enjoying the season completely free of care. You should consider taking a leaf from my book, your life would be simpler and more enjoyable, I assure you"

"You have mistaken me for someone who gives a shit" She replied and went back to her bulging bags and mutterings.

Family Argument

"It's not that you were involved with this person" Fiona said tearfully "It's that we've been married for fifteen years and the first I hear about the relationship is from that nosey cow Carmel in the golf club. I mean anyone but that Carmel, the News of the World has nothing on her when it comes to dishing the dirt. Michael, Michael, how could you put me in this position?"

"Listen sweetheart, it didn't mean anything, it's way in the past, long before we met, and it was a very brief thing anyway"

"That's easy for you to say" she cried as she slammed her wineglass down on the glass topped coffee table with a cringe making crash "Carmel also told me she saw you in the Supervalu on Thursday talking to the bitch. You never mentioned that little liaison, did you?"

"It was totally accidental darling. I'd just dropped in to get some nibbles and a bottle of Chateau Neuf du Pape, to celebrate our fifteen years of togetherness and bumped into her in the off license. I was only talking to her for two minutes if that" he said as he casually mopped his sweating brow.

"Michael" Fiona snarled in her best Cruella de Ville tone of voice "Do not take me for a complete idiot. We got married in June and its now November. Why would you choose to celebrate our anniversary five months late, and you know very well that I abhor Chateau Neuf du Pape. It gives me horrible heartburn and a miserable hangover"

"June?" Queried Michael, "Are you sure, I could have sworn that we got married later in the year. Wasn't it cold and windy on the day?

"That just puts the tin hat on it. That was your first marriage to the slut from Foxrock. Now it turns out you can't even distinguish between your wives, never mind your bits on the side. My mother warned me that it was a big mistake to get mixed up with you. Why didn't I listen to her?"

Just at this juncture the doorbell rang, and Fiona went to answer it. Michael heard her talking to the caller in the hall "Oh hello Carmel, come on in and have a drink, Michaels got some Chateau Neuf du Pape which he has just opened, I'm sure you'd like it"

Wild Ambition

"Move fast and break things, if you're not breaking things, you're not moving fast enough" Screamed Citizen Maher.

He was trying out his new persona as Master of the Universe.

"What sort of a thing is that to say?" Queried Fiona in some puzzlement. "Why would you want to break things? Random things I mean. I know very well that there's lots of things that need to be broken but just going around busting up stuff doesn't seem very productive to me"

"Fiona" Boomed his newly minted Exaltedness "You just don't get it, do you. If you want to be the head buck cat you need a slogan by which your devoted followers can readily identify you, and with which they can readily identify themselves. This move fast crack will, I guarantee, ring down the centuries to come as one of the most effective catch cries ever minted"

"It sounds as daft as a besom to me" Fiona poured cold water on his high flown rhetoric. "It might attract the riff raff of the gutter to your banner, they seem to like breaking things, whatever about moving fast, but the respectable folk won't be very turned on by it. After all the things that get broken will most likely be theirs and they won't be altogether thrilled by the spectacle of the great unwashed smashing everything they have spent their entire working life striving for"

"You really have a small mind and very limited imagination" Citizen Maher said pityingly "We don't need the supine middle class, at least in the early stages. The underprivileged masses will make great shock troops for the opening stages of our little adventure. When they've exhausted their usefulness, we can dispose of them and build a civilisation more to our liking. For that phase of the operation a strong rallying cry is absolutely critical"

"But what's wrong with 'Death to the Filthy Rich' or 'to the guillotine" Fiona did, indeed have a prosaic mind, which may be of some assistance to both her and Citizen Maher in their future incarceration in the venerable institution known as Bedlam, or the looney bin if you prefer.

Bees Knees

"You're not an adult, adults don't hide under cars and the sound you hear is not the car engine, it's the buzzing of a lone bee" Gillian had adopted a no nonsense tone in order to wield her authority over young Patrick.

Patrick was having none of it however "Feck off and leave me alone" he called over the increasingly loud buzzing "It's people like you who give adults a bad name. This bee that's under here with me is most certainly an adult because if he's flying about, he's by definition an adult and he's hiding under a car, so there"

As Patrick wriggled even further under the car to escape Gillian's attempts to dislodge him the bee spoke "Who is that annoying person and does she have to disturb the peace of a nice summer afternoon with her continuous caterwauling?"

"That's my big sister Gillian" replied Patrick, not at all phased by the fact that the bee was talking to him "She's a bossy sort at the best of times. Tell the truth I crawled under here to get away from her. I really should have known better" and he wriggled to find a more comfortable position.

"I could go out and sting her" The bee offered "That might shut her up, or at least she might go indoors for some treatment"

"But wouldn't that kill you? I was always told that if a bee stings you, he dies shortly after. She is a right royal pain in the arse, but I wouldn't like you to sacrifice yourself just to make her go away. Peace and quiet is desirable, but not at any price"

"Patrick" Gillian's shrill voice echoed off the undercarriage of the car "Who are you talking to under there? Don't make me get down on my knees in the dirt to check you out. These are my new jeans and if I get them dirty, I'll be very annoyed"

"If you must know, I'm talking to the bee. He's a much more interesting conversationalist than you are and much nicer company also. He wants to sting you and I'm trying to dissuade him but I'm not sure how long I can hold him back. You do have a very annoying voice you know"

"Ah bugger it" snarled the bee "I've had enough of her lip" and he zoomed out from under the car. Immediately Patrick heard panicked screaming from Gillian.

"The poor sad bee" He muttered, scrambling out into the daylight.

Hells Bells

Deleting the old woman's number, Beelzebub rubbed his hands together gleefully and rushed to start up his Demonbike.

"That old bitch has escaped my domain for a hundred and ten years and now she's popped her clogs. I'd say Thank God but as him and me are sworn enemies it'd hardly be appropriate. I've had her logged into my system so long I thought she'd become embedded in it forever" He crowed and danced a merry little jig.

As the Demonbike roared up to the old woman's door and screeched to a halt amidst a cloud of black smoke and a stench of Sulphur, Beezle, as he is known to his intimate group of buddies noticed to his extreme irritation a figure dressed in shining white coming into view around a nearby corner.

"What are you doing here?" He demanded, "this oul bat is mine. I've been watching her for over a century now and she's never done a kind deed in all that time, in fact her proud boast was that she never did a good deed if there was a chance of a bad one in the offing. So, shove off back to your harp plucking and your cloud sitting and let me get on with the business of gathering up her blackened and withered soul"

"Ah well you see" began the white clad figure, whom Beezle now identified as the Archangel Michael, "You of all people must be familiar with the old Catholic idea of a deathbed conversion. The man upstairs has reason to suppose that that's exactly what we have here"

Driven to the epitome of dementedness as he saw the prospect of his long awaited victim escaping his clutches Beezle screamed mightily, displaying a fine set of red tinged fangs.

"What sort of a farrago of nonsense is this?" He demanded "she has been a wicked oul whore's boot all her hundred and ten years and you reckon you can pull a stunt involving a well outdated rule from a well discredited church to help her escape her just desserts? Not on yer nelly. Now get out of my way and I won't be forced to blast you back into the lap of old white beard above"

"I think you've perhaps forgotten the last little bout we had several millennia ago" Said Michael in a soft and gentle voice "Unless my memory fails me, I royally kicked your arse back then and I haven't lost any of my edge since. So, I wouldn't be throwing my weight around here if I were you"

A Fishy Tale

"You are an ugly looking fish, aren't you" challenged Fred.

"It's imbeciles like you that gets people like me a bad name" snapped Felicity "I used to be a perfect lady until I met up with you. My mammy always told me that it's better to keep your trap shut than it is to insult someone"

"Whoa!" Fred gasped as he staggered back from the aquarium wall "You can talk!"

"Of course, I can talk" retorted Felicity "Who did you think was talking, the octopus in the corner tank? Any bleedin' fool could tell you that octopuses can't talk. Their mouths aren't shaped right for talking"

"No but" stammered Fred "As far as I'm aware nobody knows that any fish can talk. Are you unique in that respect or are there others like you?"

"Well it depends on what you mean by talk. The dogfish can bark, and the catfish can meow but that hardly constitutes conversation. To answer your question, it's mostly the more highly evolved species that have mastered the art of speech. My family tree is in the millions of years old so we're very well able to speak but we're also well up on all of the three Rs. I am regarded in literary circles as an accomplished poet and playwright but owing to the prejudices of the accursed humans, who control access to the media" I have to publish under a pseudonym. You may have heard of me?" and she mentioned a name which was eminently recognised, even by Fred, who is, it must be admitted, something of a cultural ignoramus.

"Hold on a cotton pickin' minute" cried Fred "You could make a bleedin' fortune on the celebrity circuit. The talk shows would beat a gold plated and Jewel strewn path to your door if they knew about you. A talking, poetic, playwrighting fish, my God, you'd be a sensation. You could make millions"

"Don't be any more thick than God made you" Sneered Felicity with a curled up lip "it's bad enough thank you being cooped up in this fish tank, on view to the great unwashed but you want me to go on the talk show circuit. Get real, ya dope"

So focused was Fred on the vision of multiple millions to be gained from Felicity that he failed to notice Octo the octopus until he found himself enmeshed in his tentacles.

"Well done Octo" Cried Felicity "That's the third one this week. Just drag him into my tank and we can dine high again. We should do this more often"

Ovine Golfer

"Why are there sheep on the golf course?" Demanded the stout man in the unbecoming plus fours.

"Why not, as far as my experience goes, they would make incomparably better use of it than most of the golfers I know" Replied James.

"Alternatively," he continued "A better use for a golf course might be the site of a landing ground for interplanetary spaceships with wearied travellers, fatigued from the multi century long journeys which they will have endured. After all they are human too, just like the rest of us.

Then again there may be some xenophobes amongst us who have an unreasonable objection to little green men arriving in the unsullied pastures normally reserved for those sad individuals whose primary aim in life appears to be to follow a little ball around a very large field, determined to force it into an equally little hole, for some reason explicable only to themselves.

There are, of course many, many, homeless people in the world and a different use for the said fields could be to clothe them in arctic grade tents in which the aforesaid homeless could be housed. Needless to state, there would be a need for considerable infrastructure to be installed also but this is not, in itself, a bad thing. Think of the loads of construction jobs involved in providing such infrastructure. Further jobs could be provided in other areas of the project, such as security, maintenance etc. A true win, win situation.

Marijuana is growing in popularity, If you will pardon the pun, and I'm told that it has several medical applications. I'm quite sure that with Ireland's excellent growing climate that there is a huge business potential in planting the weed on some, or all, of these patently under utilised acres of land. We could develop a thriving export trade in pot and its derivatives and together with the extra employment benefits, the foreign capital inflow has the potential to be absolutely huge.

Now I am sure that there would be a caucus of objections to any or all of these eminently sensible suggestions, but realistically speaking, how many golfers are there about, anyway?"

Bum Gig

"Being a vassal in this hole of desolation is a bum gig" Said Sigmund Bigod. "I'm sure that if I walked the walls of the whole world, I'd find a worse fiefdom, but it would be a difficult task because this is about the crappiest Fiefdom I've ever heard of, never mind come across"

"For Odin's sake man" Cried his fellow churl Olaf Olafsson "Watch what you say, the walls around here actually have ears" and he pointed his cutthroat razor at the plethora of ears decorating the walls of the small buthan where he was trying to shave in front of a fragmented mirror haphazardly stuck to the wall with what looked suspiciously like spit.

Sigmund grimaced ferociously and snarled "We needn't worry ourselves about those ears, the original owners are long dead and gone to their just reward. Old King Ethelred used to collect them from his slain enemies when he went raiding down in England and Ireland. Now there was a chieftain you'd be glad to be sworn to, raiding all summer long, loads of loot to carry home and the women! This current King is a useless wretch, always ready with a bullshit story as to why we can't go Viking anymore"

"By the way" He continued "What's with the shaving anyway? None of the girls in this crappy fiefdom would look sideways at a landless churl like you if your beard was down to your toes or if your face was as smooth as a baby's arse. Our best bet is to up sticks and go looking for a chieftain with fire in his belly and a good longship to go Viking in. Then we'd get all the girls we'd ever want"

"Sigmund, Sigmund" His companion said "You've been playing that tune for the last five years or more. So far all you do is sit around in this hovel and moan about our ill fortune. You really need to either piss or get off the pot. That young fella, Erik the Red is looking for hardy fellows to go Viking with him this season, what say we head off over to his holding and sign on"

"The stories I hear about him don't fill me with confidence" mumbled Sigmund "He's well stuck into this place he calls Greenland but from tales I hear in the Inn in town there's precious little Green about it. Nine months of year it's under four feet of snow and the other three months it's a mosquito infested swamp. Now Ireland, that'd be a different story, but it seems to have fallen out of favour lately, must be the Brian Boru fella down there. Next year maybe?"

Aces High

"I'll see your ten and raise you thirty" he said, impassively.

"It's a bit embarrassing but I don't have the thirty on me at the moment, would you accept my IOU?" I asked, feeling a bit foolish.

"A verbal contract isn't worth the paper it's printed on and an IOU in a poker game is about as much use. So ante up or fold, either is good as far as I'm concerned" The other members of the poker school looked a bit disconcerted by his brusque manner but if he was adamant that we play strictly by the rules then he was well within his rights.

Somewhat reluctantly I said "I do actually have the deeds for a castle in Donegal upstairs in my room. Would you be prepared to take them as a guarantee of my ability to pay up tomorrow?"

Snorting disgustedly, he snarled "What in God's name do I want with the deeds to a castle in Donegal? I was only in Donegal once in my life and it was a boring desolate, wet weekend. The last place on earth I'd want a castle would be Donegal. Mind you, I wouldn't want a castle anyway" here he paused and looked pensive "I'd hate to be petty, however, bring on the deeds and let's get this hand finished with"

As I went upstairs, I had time to reconsider my situation. My brother James was going to be right royally pissed off with me if, and when he heard of the proposed transaction, but the pot was enormous, well into the thousands and all my cash, and some of James's was on the table. The castle, on the other hand, was a roofless ruin standing on two acres of scraggy, rocky land exposed to the screaming gales which howled in off the Atlantic and was worth, at its most generous valuation, about five and nine pence ha'penny. On the other hand it was the last relic of old decency, handed down from our O'Neill ancestors and James had an unnatural veneration for it. If I lost it he would be upset, to say the least.

Reluctantly bearing the deeds down I threw them on the table and said "How's that? I'll see your thirty"

He grinned evilly and turned over his cards, showing a full house of aces and kings "Beat that" he crowed, maliciously.

I showed my three queens just as James shouted from the front door, "Hi, I'm home. How's it going, anything strange or startling while I was out"

Working Girl?

It's not easy loving a loser like Johnny but living with him was just the pits. It had been all lemonade and rare gas at first but his chronic inability to hold down a paying job had finally gotten beyond a joke.

His first job, when we originally got married was a commodities broker in the Bank of Ireland and we all know how that ended up!

Next up he proposed that we rent a small holding in Kerry and grow weed and magic mushrooms. I was so naive and innocent that I thought these were going to be the ingredients for an own brand soup which he would make, and I would sell at country markets on Saturdays.

The remainder of the week we would, in my mind, spend making mad passionate love and babies in our remote hideaway. The drug squad put an abrupt stop to my youthful foolishness.

The judge, taking pity, no doubt, on my tender age and Johnny's obvious stupidity imposed a suspended sentence, which hung over our heads for two long years, blighting any chance we might have of finding gainful employment. Apparently convicted drug pushers are not, generally, considered a good employment prospect.

One menial job led to another culminating in a short stint with a zero hours contract in Tesco, stacking shelves. And that was my career path. Johnny was far too refined and full of his own importance to descend to this level so instead he went on the scratcher. That lasted about three months until they found out that he had fraudulently claimed for a wife and three kids, two boys and a girl.

Needless to remark the social didn't take kindly to Johnny's version of entrepreneurship. He was cut off without the proverbial shilling and was informed that he should consider himself lucky that he was not charged and sent to prison.

Things finally reached the breaking point when he proposed that he was ideally suited to the position of pimp. He had a habit of lying in bed until afternoon and staying out all night with disreputable people, furthermore he was, undeniably good looking and extremely charming, all useful attributes for the person desirous of having this highly sought after position.

I was, not too surprisingly, less than enthusiastic about this idea, but when he proposed that I become his first working girl I rebelled absolutely.

With a disgruntled expression my husband slid two twenty dollar bills across the table, "That's all we have left" he said "Have you a better idea? That was the last straw.

Talebearer

Blabber Mouth

Maggie couldn't keep the secret any longer, she just had to tell Mitchell.

"Why did you tell me that. I could have quite happily gone the rest of my life without hearing shit like that" Mitchell was not at all impressed with Maggie's blabbermouth.

"But I needed to share with someone. If I didn't tell somebody, I'd have burst. This is too big a story to keep to myself"

"Yeah, but what did I do to deserve your misplaced confidence? I hate secrets, I can't keep one to save my life. Now I have this shit stuck on the forefront of my mind and I won't be able to sleep easy until I pass it on to some other unfortunate"

"God no, you can't pass it on, it's a secret, don't you understand the concept of a secret? Blabbing it around just dilutes it and soon it's devalued like the Chilean Bolivar. You need to swear you'll keep shtumm about it. Go on, promise on your mother's life"

"My mother is dead these twenty years, what would be the point of promising on her life, for God's sake. If I was forced to swear, I'd rather choose something meaningful"

"Meaningful? Like what? The beard of the Prophet? The Ten Commandments? Come on, think of something, I'm seriously worried that the minute you leave me you'll be blabbing to the first person you meet. Everyone will know that the story had to come from me. Nobody will ever trust me with a confidence again. I have my reputation to consider you know"

"I could swear on our undying friendship, that might do the trick. What do you think?"

"Oh, bloody hell, if that's the best you can do! Get on with it then and I'll see you in Mooneys tomorrow night"

Ten minutes later Mitchell met Nancy, "Nancy" He crowed "you won't believe what Maggie just told me!"

Monopoly Money

My life changed when I found that huge envelope stuffed with cash in the coupon exchange bucket at the supermarket.

Sadly, when I went to spend it the bloody stuff was Monopoly money.

"Who" I wondered "would be so base as to play a horrible joke like that on an innocent passerby like myself"

Grinding my teeth in rage, I turned away from the cash desk, leaving my enormous pile of luxury items scattered on the bagging tray. No yellow pack trash for me if I'm flush.

Suddenly I noticed two young boys, consumed with helpless laughter just by the vegetable shelves.

"Did you pair leave that duff cash in the coupon exchange bucket?" I demanded, now in a towering rage.

"Ah, jeez man," the taller one chortled "You should have seen the state of yourself when you saw the envelope full of folding green. I thought for a minute that you'd have a heart attack. The big red face and the shifty eyes looking around to see if anyone had copped you. It was the funniest thing since me granny got run over by the number fourteen bus"

"I've a good mind to get both of you charged with conduct likely to lead to a breach of the peace, cause, right now I feel a breach of the peace coming on"

"Ooh, Billy we better run away, I don't know about you but the skinny little old man in the shabby clothes is scaring me. I hope he doesn't nag me to death, because he doesn't exactly seem too dangerous otherwise" This creep was cruising for a bruising.

"Well" I said, drawing a desert eagle pistol (the biggest handgun in the world) from under my coat "My old friend Mr Colt here might be of some assistance in teaching you pair that actions sometimes have consequences"

The taller one fainted dead away and his companion, Billy, dropped to his knees pleading "Please Mr, it wasn't me. Pauly there got the idea when he got the Monopoly set from his Auntie for Christmas. He never saw a game like that before and he only likes digital games so he decided that he might as well get some fun out of the money. I swear that we'll never do anything like that again as long as we live, cross me heart and hope to die we won't"

Patting the lad on the shoulder and assuming my proper Superman guise I said "OK, son pick up your buddy and don't let me see you hanging around the Supermarket again"

Pugilism

Killer Maguire was well on his way to the top of the tree in the pugilism stakes in Ireland, Europe and he had ambitions for America and the world next year.

His major headache was the support staff such an ambitious task would call for. His manager, Cauli O'Brien, so called because of his badge of honour from his own, not so stellar past in the ring, his malformed cauliflower ears, would, of course remain with him.

He had, after all, given Killer his first break way back when he was a teenager in a dingy gym in Mullinahone, and Killer could not envisage a bout without Cauli in his corner. His business manager Frank was a different prospect, however.

Disturbing rumours had come to Killer's notice concerning Frank's propensity for dipping his hand into the takings, not to an enormous extent, you understand, but enough to have become noticeable, and enough to be a worry, nonetheless. Killer knew that he would have to confront Frank at some point, but he really didn't like confrontation, so he decided to put off this painful discussion until a future date.

There was another issue also. Every successful pugilist requires, as a matter of necessity, a dollop of arm candy with which he could be seen around town in nightclubs and other social haunts gazing adoringly into each other's eyes and having their pictures taken by the paparazzi for the delectation of the chattering classes.

Killer had noticed a distinct cooling in his relationship with Peaches Montez recently and was unsure of the reasons for this rift within the lute of love, but as with Frank, he was unsure of how to proceed with dealing with the matter. It would undoubtedly sort itself out in due course, he supposed.

Of far greater import for Killer was the behaviour of the guy who waited in his corner during rounds. Paddy, for such was his name, has also been with Killer since God was a boy, but recently something seemed to be awry with him. He was no longer as energetic at waving the towel in Killers face or in offering the water bottle between rounds as he had been before. And he had become forgetful also.

Only yesterday he had laid out red shorts for Killer's bout with Fancy Dancer Finnegan. Everyone in the boxing fraternity knows very well that red shorts are an invitation to disaster.

This was an issue which Killer could not ignore. It is a little known fact that the guy in the corner is vital to the successful outcome of any boxing event.

"It's me belly" Paddy replied when Killer asked him what was wrong "I have a pain in me belly and I'm afraid to go to the Doctor because you never know what can happen in a second's belly"

At the Swimming Pool

Davy Jones decided that he needed to indulge in some physical exercise. He had long been a follower of Henry Ford's dictum 'When I feel the urge to exercise, I lie down until the urge goes away'

A long lifetime of eating doughnuts, both fresh and stale had left him distinctly pudgy. This condition was not helped by his sedentary lifestyle, in fact sedentary probably did not fit the bill, comatose might be nearer the mark. However, his cardiologist had persuaded him otherwise.

Having paid his money and dressed himself in his, totally last decades, speedos he ventured out to the pool area.

He decided he would impress the other two old gentlemen and the middle aged lady in the pool with his diving prowess, this despite the clear demand displayed prominently everywhere that such behaviour was severely discouraged.

Cleaving the water with scarcely a ripple Davy found himself heading for the bottom somewhat more precipitously than he had anticipated. As he approached the bottom, he found himself being dragged even faster into a vortex centred on the huge drain hole at the base of the pool.

"Oh dear" he thought "This can't be good. I'm a fairly good swimmer but if I get sucked in here, I probably won't survive to tell the tale"

Try as he might and despite his herculean struggles he was drawn helplessly down into the maw of the vortex.

As he slipped into the drain hole, which to him bore a striking resemblance to a grinning mouth, and just before he blacked out, his last thoughts were of motherhood and apple pie and dear old Ireland.

To his astonishment he woke up in a greenish tinted grotto surrounded by a bevy of beautiful mermaids.

"This is a bit of alright" he thought "I wonder if this is the afterlife? I never heard of mermaids in the afterlife but maybe if you die by drowning you get greeted by these beauties, more or less as a sort of compensation? Anyway, let's just lie back and see how things go"

The leader of the denizens of this underwater habitat called to one of the others "Look what just washed down to us. It's a long time since we had such a prime specimen, prepare for a grand celebration and get the place ready for a feast"

"Ah no, you don't have to put yourselves out for me" Davy cried "Mind you a cup of coffee and a fish finger sandwich would go down a treat, I'm a bit peckish after my traumatic experience"

"Don't be silly" Replied the head mermaid "The feast is for us, and you, are the main course"

Dictator

Poor Adolf Schicklegruber, born with a name like that, what chance in life did he have?

School must have been a torment to the unfortunate kid. "Hey Schickeles, gimme your lunch money or I'll punch the living day lights out of you" You can almost hear the taunts, can't you?

And his time in the army! The enormous, Prussian drill Sergeant screaming at the small, short sighted lad whose one aim in life was to get by under the radar. The fact that he achieved the rank of corporal speaks volumes about his inner strength and fortitude.

It's not clear when he changed his name but the genius of choosing Hitler as a surname surely answers the query "What's in a name?" Following that life changing decision his rise to the dizzying heights of his later, short, life was nothing short of mesmeric.

Admittedly some of his decisions were a little wrongheaded, invading Poland and France was possibly not the sharpest move, but he did drag Germany back from the deepest recession experienced by any nation before or since.

He was also, if we are to believe the stories, devoted to his dog. Nobody who is devoted to his dog can be all bad, can they?

Attacking the Russian bear was certainly well up there as one of the worst blunders in military history. Taking on the most populous nation in Europe with a history of scant regard for its own citizens' welfare, and in Winter too. Not clever.

The reasons for his hatred of the Jewish people are unclear. Was it just that he coveted their wealth and influence? Certainly, there is a long history of Jewish persecution in Europe for those very reasons. He was also most likely badly advised in this matter by others in his kitchen cabinet. Goebbels, Bormann and Goring are names which spring to mind.

For my money the old saying which my mother used to quote seems apt:

There's a little bit of good in the worst of us,

And a little bit of bad in the best of us,

And as good as you are,

And as bad as I am

You're as bad as I am,

As good as you are!

Sing for your Supper

"Jaysus" she croaked "how could this happen on today of all days? It's the finals for the Voice of Ireland and I've been practicing for the past year for it"

Boom, in a puff of smoke an imp from hell appeared in front of her, "My infernal master has bidden me to invite you to visit with him. He apologises that he is otherwise engaged at this moment, if not he would have come here himself. Apparently, you are in some difficulties and he would like to make you an offer you can't refuse, if you know what I mean"

"Oh shit" she thought "Not the old 'Your immortal soul for your greatest wish' bullshit! I thought that went out with high button boots"

Opening a window and switching on a fan to disperse the sulphurous vapours emanating from her uninvited guest she asked "What does your infernal master want with me? I don't even believe in him or the other guy with the long white beard and snowy nightshirt. I really don't think that any of these guys can sort out a strep throat in time for tonight's gig. And it's on telly too with maybe a million viewers tuned in" With this last comment a lonely tear slid down her cheek and a heartrending sob escaped her.

"You might be agreeably surprised about what my glorious leader can do" Replied the imp, imps don't have names, especially Christian names, that would be just weird, so he couldn't introduce himself properly "Why don't you just hold my hot little hand and we'll pop off down and have a chat with his demonic majesty, after all things can hardly get any worse than they are at present now, can they?"

Grasping his hand, which was indeed, both little and hot, she was immediately transported with a gratifying boom into the nether regions. To her considerable surprise she found that hell was exactly like she had always seen it portrayed, hot, steamy and with a ruddy cast to the atmosphere. It was not improved by the intense stink of sulphur either.

"Welcome, welcome, welcome" Boomed the voice of the big cheese of the underworld "Sorry I couldn't be on hand to transport you down here myself; I had the ex chairman of the CRC in my office being interviewed for a position in my organisation and it went on longer than expected. In the final end I had to tell him that he was unwelcome here, his demands for salary and pension rights were simply excessive. If he'd been paid what he demanded he'd have been bringing home more than me, and that's not on, know what I mean?"

With a start our heroine woke up and drawing her hand across his sweating brow she said "I knew I shouldn't have eaten that stinking bishop cheese for supper last night"

Shaggy Dog Story

My trip to the grocery store was uneventful, but as I turned onto my street, I noticed the police cars surrounding my house

"Dear God" I thought "Not Snuffles, don't let anything have happened to Snuffles. I don't think I could carry on without Snuffles"

Rushing up to the man who seemed to be in charge with tears streaming down my face I pleaded "Please tell me it's not Snuffles; I only went around the corner to get some doggy treats. I've only been gone a few minutes" and I burst into heartrending sobs.

"Get a grip on yourself Woman commanded the man who seemed to be familiar to me "We have more important things to be thinking about than a mangy dog here"

"Snuffles isn't a dog you big bully, he's my pet mole. And he's very sensitive, so he is. Don't you dare to compare him to a mangy dog" As I spoke it dawned on me why the man looked familiar, "He's the guy who's been all over the telly this past couple of weeks" I thought "The politician fellow, yeah the Minister for Injustice. That's the one"

"Just what do you think is going on here" I demanded, collecting my courage in both hands "You can't just block the street and barricade honest upstanding citizens pets in their houses without a good reason"

"My good woman" The smarmy git started,

"Don't you give me that My Good Woman guff, I'm nobody's good woman, and I'm most certainly not your Good Woman. Any more of that crap out of you and I'll deck you with my handbag. I mean it, now get out of my way and let me in my house"

"Madam" He opened his mouth to speak, then paused as he saw me raise my, not inconsiderable handbag "Please restrain yourself we have a matter of national security in hand here, we've had a report that terrorists are inhabiting your house and we must ensure that they are apprehended and brought before the law"

"Terrorists is it, you big gobshite, there's nobody but me and Snuffles living in the house. Now will you get out of my way and let me check on him. The poor dear must be terrified out of his little mind. You're the only terrorist around here. You should know that moles are timid creatures and easily upset"

"Moles! what did you say, there's a mole in your house? Sergeant what exactly did that anonymous call say again?"

Superbug

"Bloody Hell, just as I start my Superman career my bleedin' diverticulitis starts to act up. You'd think a man of steel would be able to get through a day without having to spend half of it sitting down on the crapper. I'm giving up on this gig, right now" Clark Kent was seriously put out.

"Ah now, supie, don't be such a drama queen. Surely you're not going to let a little tummy upset call a halt to your new venture as the defender of all that's pure and good in America, firstly and after that the unenlightened parts of the world outside the Continental United States" Said Lex Luthor "Besides, who would I have as my arch enemy if you pack it up? Spider-Man is a wimp, Batman and Robin are involved in a deep relationship and they have no time for chasing criminals and as for the Famous Four, well the less said about them the better"

"Oooh, the pain" Groaned poor old Superman, "Nobody in the history of the world has suffered like this. That evil bastard, The Joker, must have laced my breakfast porridge with Kryptonite, that's the only explanation for this condition. After all I have the original iron constitution, yeah, that's it Kryptonite"

"This too shall pass" boomed Aquaman from the outdoor pool "I've seen this sort of thing happen before. All it needs is a large dose of motilium, that'll sort it and you can get on with your crime fighting gig"

Bacchus had been hanging around in the back of the room throughout this conversation, now you might be wondering where he fits in this story, but after all the Greek Gods were the original super heroes and he was a God so, ipso facto he's in.

"In my considerable experience, and I've had considerable experience of the aftereffects of overindulgence, the best thing of all is a tincture of good brandy, it's a sovereign cure for all ills, despite what the Irish might say about Uisce Beatha"

All were stricken into silence when Martha, Superman's mammy arrived carrying a bowl of corn flour cooked in milk.

"Sit down alanna" she crooned and spooning the mixture into his open mouth she commenced to sing an ancient Irish lullaby.

"Ah, mammy" Superman cried "That's just the ticket, how did you know I was hurting?"

"Son, a mammy always knows" she said with a loving smile.

Pirate Woes

Although spring had sprung the week before, winter had now returned with a vengeance. Given that the weather was inclement for pirating Arthur decided to finally get down to writing his long delayed letter home to his mother.

Dear Mother,

I am writing to let you know that I am doing well in my profession as a Pirate. Please, when replying to this letter address me as Black Jack, as my given name would be a source of amusement and bullying. My fellow pirates are not well known for their gentility and Arthur the Pirate somehow doesn't give the right vibe.

As you know I ran away from home some fifteen years ago and signed on as a cabin boy on a ship bound for the West Indies. I am sorry it took so long for me to write to you, but I have been somewhat otherwise occupied until now.

Our vessel the Saucy Jane, was attacked by pirates on the Spanish Main and all aboard were put to the sword save me and the captain's mongrel dog. Fortunately for me there was a vacancy for a cabin boy aboard the pirate vessel "The Black Swan" and I was given the choice of walking the plank or joining up. Not being stupid I chose the latter option.

The pirate leader "Redbeard O'Shaughnessy" put me to work as a Jack of all trades and warned me that my continued existence depended on swift and competent responses to his orders and an ability to learn the trade of pirating quickly.

After a long career in the Swan, I rose to captain my own vessel "Naughty Nancy" and for a number of years ploughed a very successful furrow up and down the Caribbean. Unfortunately, as you pointed out to me on many occasions in my youth "Into every life a little rain must fall" and in my case a veritable waterfall of disasters has crashed down upon me.

Last year the King, God Bless Him, sent a new Governor to the colonies and he arrived with all the enthusiasm of a new broom. He galvanised the formerly lethargic Royal Navy garrison and put them to the task of cleaning up the piracy situation in the region.

I now find myself in durance vile in His Majesty's prison in Kingston town, condemned to hang as a buccaneer within the next three months. My only hope is to bribe my jailer and flee into the rain forest. Unfortunately, all the treasure which I gained during my career was dissipated on wine, women and song and I do not have the wherewithal to pay the usurious vermin.

Please Mother, if you can find it in your heart to send money, I will be forever grateful.

Your loving Son,

Arthur.

Argonauts at Sea

Jason said it was an accident, but was it, really...

"It wasn't my fault" Jason whined "How was I supposed to know that Hercules would leave his blasted short sword there? Nobody in his right mind would leave a sharp implement under the rowing benches would they. And anyway, how is it my fault if Persephone snuck aboard dressed as a boy? Everybody knows that women are the worst of bad luck on board a boat"

"Listen you plank" Screeched Persephone "Though it's probably a compliment to call you a plank. In the present circumstances a plank would be a useful thing" Tears streamed from her eyes as she looked at the enormous geyser of cold seawater erupting through to gaping hole in the keel of the good ship Argo. "It was you who poked the sword through the bottom of the boat"

"It's no good everyone getting their togas in a twist" Said Theseus "We're in a bit of a pickle here and we need to do something about it. Has any of you guys got any carpentry experience?"

Castor and Pollux, those pestilential twins, speaking as one said "You'd think with a crew of eighty five able bodied men and one woman that someone would be at least adequate in woodwork, especially aboard ship"

The eminent shipbuilder Argus was conspicuous by his lack of contribution to the conversation. As the original builder of the ship, he might have been expected to have some thoughts on the needed repair. However, he was a dry land shipbuilder first and last. He didn't do underwater repairs.

Erginus, son of Poseidon, Greek God of the sea said with a casual wave of his hand "I'm off to visit with my Daddy. See you suckers later" And he dived overboard.

The remainder of the crew gathered to discuss their plight and their response to it. Finally, it was decided that they would take turns sitting in the hole until they could reach land and have Argus fix the leak.

Sadly, when it came to her turn, Persephone, always ready to be awkward, declaimed "I'm not doing that, it's just not ladylike" And she stormed off to sulk in the bilges.

The male crew then agreed and adopted the position with as good grace as they could muster.

And that, children, is why, to this day, men stand with their arse to the fire at every opportunity.

Kidnapped

Now that I've got him tied up in the basement, the next step is to demand some dough for his return.

What's a nice round number? I'm not sure this was the best thought out scheme in the world. I meant to get Joe, you know, the guy who gets all those calls on the radio in the afternoon, yeah, that's right, Joe Duffy, but some woman at the bus stop told me that this guy was him.

This gink doesn't seem to have much going for him, he's retired on a small pension and he has notions about being a writer but to tell the God's truth he hasn't two halfpennies to rub off a tombstone.

I know! I'll tweet Enda Kenny and tell him that if he doesn't cough up a million Euro, I'll do the old guy a damage and dump him on the steps of Leinster House. Enda's a nice person with the milk of human kindness flowing in his veins so no doubt he'll be happy to shell out.

Bloody hell, here it is in the papers, Enda's out of the country representing the EU in Uzbekistan or Kazakhstan or one of those stans off over there wherever. He won't be back for ages and he'll most likely be knackered after his travels. No point in troubling him then.

Eamonn Gilmore? Nah he's a tight arsed git like all the rest of the smoked salmon socialists.

I could try Gerry Adams but with his past I'm more likely to have an Armalite shoved in my face than a bag of money in my hand.

Mick Wallace now, there's a decent sort. He wouldn't see someone stuck for a few bob, sure if he hadn't got it handy he could ask the revenue guys to give him a bit of an advance on his salary. Or maybe not?

Bertie Ahern, there's a man who understands the need for a dig out. But he's retired now and living on a pension himself. He might find it difficult to lay his hand on a cool mil.

All this concentration on politicians is most probably not the best thing. Let's give the celebs a shout.

There's Bono now, he's got more money than God. I wonder if he's on twitter. I know he lives out in Killiney but with the new property tax he might be a bit strapped just now.

The three Seans; Dunne, Quinn and Fitzpatrick are well stuck with NAMA after them for their last shilling so they're a dead number

My bloody head is reeling with this whole thing!

Here you, here's the bus fare home. Go on now and good night to you!

Heroes for a Day

"We can be heroes, just for one day" - David Bowie

"If David Bowie said it, who am I to disagree" said Kevin as he sat on the dunes in Ballybunion contemplating the current state of his existence.

He had been engaged by a lady of uncertain age to surveil her husband whom she was convinced had been seduced from the path of virtue by virago from the wilds of West Kerry. He had produced as a feeble excuse for his desire to go to the butt end of the universe a desire to study the mating habits of the common tern.

Given that the bird in question, as evidenced by its title was common to all the coasts of Ireland the necessity to travel so far from the bosom of his, admittedly small family, the couple had not been blessed by children, when the said tern could be found in plenteous profusion in his own backyard in sunny Kilbarrack gave the whole story an unlikely flavour, to be charitable about it.

So, Kevin found himself semi concealed in the marram grass on the dunes of the Ballybunion foreshore. He was a fairly recent convert to this gumshoe business but despite his relative inexperience he was fairly convinced that the business of the Seabird in question was very far from the errant husband's mind. He had gotten his first clue when he had been rudely awakened in his B&B by the banging of the next door headboard on the adjoining wall and the loud calling on the name of the deity by the aforesaid virago, together with her loud use of the husband's name repeated in ever increasing volume until the abrupt cessation of all sound from the room next door.

He had deliberately booked the room in question in order to further his investigations, but he had not really expected such an immediate and graphic confirmation of his client's suspicions.

Now he watched as the pair cavorted in the waves crashing on the beach, displaying all the signs of innocent enjoyment of the facilities offered by the neighbourhood.

"Mind you" Kevin mused "I wouldn't mind playing the hero with her myself, even if it was only for one day"

Euromillions

That's my numbers, I cried to myself. It's a multi million jackpot. I'm set for life.

The second thought that sprang into my mind was "What'll I do now?" I have somewhat more than I need to keep body and soul together.

To quote Mr Micawber 'Annual income twenty pounds, annual expenditure nineteen pounds, nineteen shillings and sixpence, result: Happiness. Annual expenditure twenty pounds and sixpence, result: Misery.

Using the Micawber scale, I figured that I was firmly in the first category and really didn't need an obscene wedge of money. On the other hand, there are a lot of things you can do with multiple millions, so just what?

First off, I could give the kids a million apiece, just to set them up like. Then I could buy an ocean going yacht, complete with captain and crew. Maybe a personal jet, just so I don't have to queue for Ryanair ever again. Then I could send my cruiser to the Caribbean and fly out after it without having to endure the long ocean journey. At the other end I'd really need a villa of my own, no point in staying with the Hoi polloi in some five star hotel.

I might consider giving some of my filthy lucre to the poor and the needy, but on the other hand, what did the poor and the needy ever do for me? Naw, on mature reflection stuff the poor and the needy.

All that done, I'd hire a team of accountants and lawyers to ensure that none of my hard earned dosh fell into the hands of the Revenue Commissioners. We've all seen how they manage to squander money on idiotic stuff like education and health etc. anyway it's a given that the obscenely rich don't pay taxes.

Then I could sit back, relax and watch the dividends roll in. As Eartha Kitt famously sang "In my cottage there would be, a soundproof nursery, not to wake the babies while I'm counting.

Unfortunately, or otherwise, when I stuck the ticket in the machine to check it went Blaah no luck! So, back to the drawing board.

Loves Labour Lost

Gazing in confusion at the unlabelled can I reached into the cigarette pack which contained my stash of M&Ms and withdrew the red coloured one. Red M&Ms are my favourite sort. Sighing profoundly, I pondered the vagaries of human nature.

Why oh, why did Felicity reject my advances so persistently. It's not like she could be in any doubt as to how deeply my feelings for her went. I had been plying her with costly gifts for months now and in every case she had returned them unopened. Talk about unrequited love!

Last week I had sent her an exquisitely bound copy of the Book of Kells, I happen to know that she's big into that class of thing and I figured that if iconography by mouldy old monks, long dead and gone, was her bag, then I'd play on that.

Personally, if I wanted to study the bible I think I'd take the King James Version, at least it's legible. The Colmcille version is just so much hard work to me. Still if that's what it takes?

My curiosity was raging about the unlabelled can. It was part of a job lot I'd bought at a car boot sale in Fairyhouse last year, I mean, if you can't trust a Meath car boot salesman, who can you trust? To date the whole unlabelled can thing was proving about as fruitful as my pursuit of Felicity. All of those that I had opened to date had contained pickled beetroot. I'm not sure what others might think about pickled beetroot but to me it's the bottom pit of vegetable hell. I cordially dislike pickled vegetables at the best of times and hate, with a purple passion, beetroots, but pickled beetroots? The less said about them the soonest mended.

Now some of you may be wondering what the connection is between my hopeless pursuit of Felicity and my vain quest for satisfaction in the two dozen unlabelled cans. Simply put, one is a metaphor for the other. I may one day open a can and find it is full of succulent peaches and I may connect up with Felicity, she hasn't yet returned the Book of Kells after all.

But neither outcome is likely.

Conflict Resolution

There were many stories told about that battle but the strangest tale of all was Seamus's. It all started on a wet Saturday morning when Seamus rose from his bed of pain with a raging thirst and a head like a Def Metal concert.

"What in the name of the seven snotty orphans of Clonmacnoise and Glendalough was I drinking last night?" He moaned pitifully.

Struggling to open the fridge for the milk to soften his cup of ambition he discovered, not too much to his surprise that the last carton was in a state approaching cheese.

Throwing on some clothes he staggered out to the nearest ATM to replenish his wallet. imagine his surprise when he saw a large crowd surrounding the machine. Craning his neck, he saw a sign on the face of the cash dispenser "Free Cash Today" it said in large glaring letters.

Almost as soon as he emerged on the scene a fracas broke out at the front of the crowd. The melee quickly escalated into a full scale eye gouging, nail scratching, ear biting battle royal. It was every man for himself and the devil take the hindmost and the elderly lady at the back wailing. "Ah leave it out, lads" was ignored by all and sundry and only maintained her stance by the most rigorous of contortions.

As the roar reached a crescendo and the sound of approaching police sirens neared, Seamus was astonished to see a vortex opening in the middle of the ATM and a swarm of minuscule men on horseback emerging.

Swiftly laying about them with their swords of light the mini men quickly brought order from the chaos.

The leader of the cavalry stood up in his stirrups and with a stentorian roar informed all and sundry that he and his merry men had come from the land of nod to put manners on the unruly Irish.

"That's just not right" cried Seamus as he awakened from his drunken stupor "That was all too graphic. What the hell was I drinking last night?"

Filthy Lucre

Money makes the world go round.

"That's a load of old horse feathers" Maurice shouted "the world turns on its axis with or without the intervention of money, so it's going to go round whether or which. And as for the root of all evil shite, that's donkey feathers too. Money is neither intrinsically good nor bad. What makes it so is the use to which it is put"

"What's got you all steamed up all of a sudden?" his grandson Harry asked "I thought we had you safely planted nearly seventy years ago, but here you are jumping up and down and ranting about money. I would have thought you'd have better things to be thinking of, in the afterlife, than filthy lucre"

"That's easy for you to say" the spectral figure moaned "I've had to listen for decades to the fruit of my loins whinging and complaining about where the family money went. I'll tell you where it went. I spent it on wine, women and song, that's where it went. Anybody who doesn't like that answer can kiss my bony arse. So, There!"

"Jeez, Maurice, cool your jets for God's sake. If you keep on like that you'll give yourself a conniption fit. Oh, that's right, you're already dead so a conniption fit is out of the question for you, isn't it?"

Harrys wife was fond of saying that if it rained money, he'd be left as the only one in town equipped with a fork. Harry, on the other hand preferred to think that he was just not too pushed about having or not having it. On balance if it was available in abundance, well and good, if not well live with it was probably a good summation as to his attitude.

His sainted Grandfather, on the other hand, had worked hard in America to amass sufficient hard cash to come home and establish a business in Dublin. Preferably one with the name "Browne and Sons" emblazoned over the door. Sadly, for his vaulting ambition, none of his children or grandchildren, demonstrated his capacity for getting, and holding onto large quantities of moolah.

Rattling his chains, did I mention his chains earlier? Maurice receded into the infinite darkness muttering as he went:

"None of you lot had a drop of the Browne's blood in your veins. It's plain to me that the Hunters have totally corrupted any smidgeon of financial competence I might have left to you. I'm off back to where I came from!"

Cockalorum

The cockalorum, Frederick the Unwary, was confronted by two arcane objects, a golden hammer and a cup of what appeared to be water.

"What to do, what to do?" He carolled. "I must choose one or the other, but which? And do I must needs justify my choice? And if I do, to whom must I give the justification? A golden hammer might be quite useful if I was an auctioneer, employed possibly by Sotheby's. They are, after all the preeminent auctioneering company in the world. It's unlikely that they would use any of the baser metals in their gavels so having a golden one might place me higher up the list of potential future employees"

With a pensive air he continued "Judges too have gavels, don't they. As there is a hierarchy of positions in the law courts from district to supreme, presumably they too may use gavels of increasing value as they rise through the judicial ranks. Therefore, a solid gold implement might easily stand me in good stead"

"The cup of water, on the other hand, what's that all about?" He pondered "For a person of my importance and standing in the community a cup of water looks, on first inspection like a very poor choice given that the choice will determine whether I'm ready or not! Ready for what? At the same time if that which I'm ready for is, for instance an opportunity to serve on the Supreme Court Bench, then a cup of water would seem to be a poor choice, while a golden gavel, Ahhh, that would be a different kettle of fish altogether"

"But hold up a minute. What if what's in the cup is not water? What if it is the tears of a Phoenix instead? Even Harry Potter could tell you that Phoenix tears can heal all wounds and, indeed restore the dead to life. Now that would be much cooler than the Supreme Court gig. It could be a draught from the fabled Fountain of Youth in Tir na nOg, used by Oisín to prolong his life for three hundred years until he foolishly used his strength to help lift a heavy weight and fell on the cursed ground of Eireann and immediately aged catastrophically. If it's that I won't be lifting any heavy weights, no sirree!"

"All things considered I think I'll give the whole thing a miss, go down to Kavanaghs and get myself a nice creamy pint. Leave the difficult decisions to others I say"

Lost and Wandering

"The thing about being lost" Mused Billy "Is that, strictly speaking you can't be lost, because by definition you are the centre of your own universe so when someone says 'I'm lost' what they actually mean is that they have lost everything and everyone else"

"Jeez Bill" His brother Jimmy said exasperatedly "You do come up with some bullshit from time to time. People get lost all the time, sure hardly a week goes by without somcone being found wandering on the Reeks in Killarney, causing all manner of grief for the unfortunate Park Rangers who have to go out in all weathers to drag their useless arses home safe. You can't mean to suggest that it's us that's are lost in such a case as that, now can you?

"Ah well, in an existential sense, and speaking from the wanderer's perspective he knew exactly where he was at all times, it was all the rest of us who were looking for him. He may not have known his way home, but he could find himself at all times. The thing was, he couldn't find anyone else, it you follow my drift" Billy blew out a huge plume of vapour which he had sucked from his latest fad, the cursed electronic cigarette.

"Well if you're going to be like that where do you leave that comedian fella, Bill Hicks. I heard him saying on the telly last night that life is only a dream and we are the imagination of ourselves" Jimmy sneered, thinking that he had bested his brother for once.

"Bill Hicks you say" Billy filled the room with another blast from his steam machine "I must check him out, it sounds as if he might be on to something all right. I've often thought that I'm the only real person in the world and all the rest of you are figments of my imagination. I mean, I have no empirical evidence to prove that that's not the case"

"If I gave you a punch in the snot" Snarled Jimmy "You'd soon know that there was someone else in the room with you"

"But that's just the thing" Replied Billy "I could be just as easily imagining you and the punch both"

"Well that's OK then, here's an imaginary fifty Euro note for the one you loaned me last week. So, we're quits then?"

"I wouldn't take it as fast as that" said a crestfallen Billy.

Capricious Nature

There's Dorothy now, and god knows it would be a tragedy if anything made a man of her. She's just about perfect as she is, and she can only improve as time goes on. So, Mother Nature, kindly leave Dorothy alone.

The cowardly lion on the other hand, he might be a candidate. Mind you he'd be a very shaggy type of man and he'd most likely have to shave twice a day. His barber would make a fortune trimming his hair but if he went for the shaven look, he might appear very strange.

The tin man has no chance. Admittedly his abiding wish is to have a heart, but what he'd do with a heart is a bit difficult to figure out. I mean a heart is merely a pump for driving blood around the body in order to nourish the various body parts. Old Tin Man has no flesh and blood body parts so ergo! No need of a heart. In order for him to be made a man of he'd need radical remodelling, out of the question at this point in time.

Now me, I'm made of mainly natural, not to say, organic parts. You don't get much more basic than straw, after all. But it would be a very long stretch to expect the divine Gaia to transform me into a real, functioning man. There's a world of difference between straw and human body parts. Some unkind people have put about the story that I am somewhat lacking in the upper storey, but that's just not the case. You don't need ganglions and neurones to string together a couple of connected thoughts. I can form two totally contradictory thoughts at the same time as well as any meat machine.

The more I think on it, the more I'm convinced that this transformation would be the worst move I could possibly make. My parts are infinitely replaceable as long as grass grows. I don't differentiate between brain cells and any other cells. If I lose a foot, I can easily use some of my head stuffing which is not in use, whilst I head off to the corn field on a fully functioning pair of feet. And so on ad absurdiam.

So, Mother Nature can get stuffed, if she will pardon the phrase.

Poets and Lesser Mortals

"Facebook is the invention of the devil!" Mary exclaimed "Look at the lousy prompt this dipshit has just handed out, and me in a delicate frame of health after the Christmas and all"

"Now Mary" Cautioned the beloved group facilitator "That's no way to be starting the new year. If you don't like that prompt you can always try the other one, and if all else fails, you can write something unrelated to anything which went before. And if you don't like those options you can turn your arse to the whole gig, for all I care"

"Hold on now" Cried the poet "surely we can conduct our business in a civilised fashion? Please moderate your attitudes, you're wrecking my buzz here, with your negativity. How is anyone going to write some deathless literature with all this wrangling going on"

"This is typical of your arrogance" Stormed Mary "You think you're better than the rest of us because you write poetry. You never miss an opportunity to throw your poetic prowess in the faces of us lesser, prose writers. I vote we ban poets from any further meetings of our group, what say you all?"

"Ah, hang on" appealed the beloved facilitator, frantically attempting to pour oil on troubled waters whilst the poet attempted to ignite the oil as fast as it was poured "I'm quite sure our esteemed poetic member didn't mean to cast nasturtiums on other, non poet, members. I suggest it's just a mistaken impression that poets look down on us lesser mortals

"Is it hell" Snarled The poet "everyone in the literary community knows that chick lit is the lowest form of writing and poetry is the highest. Anyone who doesn't know that is just a thundering ignoramus and if you'll just give me a few minutes I'll dash off an ode to ignorance which I'll be happy to dedicate to our esteemed sister"

Happily scribbling away and totally oblivious to the storm raging around him the quietest member of the group continued writing his twelfth successful novel.

Great Expectations

Don't take offence

"If yiz wooden be castin nasturtiums I wooden be takin offence" Josie said in high dudgeon. "Some people likes coddle, follied by cake for their dinners, others doesn't. Me self I'm not fond of them fat sausages yiz get from the butchers in Dorset Street, yiz know the ones with the furrin name. Superquinn sausages is defini the best, though mind you since they changed to that new name, I'm not convinced they're the same at all"

Frank was quite puzzled as he sat beside her looking at the sign. "What's the bleeding story here" he complained "Tha sign makes no sense a all. I mean what's yer man doin with the fence and since when do road signs tell you not to do dis or da? And what's coddle got to do wir anything? I mean, if yer goin to start ramblin on abou' stuff try an keep to the bleeding point will ya"

"You know very well whar I'm talkin' abou' Frank Maguire. I made a beautiful coddle for dinner las nigh' an' you left half it on the plate behind ye'. I had te feed it to the feckin' moggie, so I did. A total waste of good food, so it was. It's a bleedin' sin to be wastin' good food, me mammy always told me" She was obviously well up on her high horse by now.

"Yeah bu what's Tha' got ta do with the bleedin' sign" Whined Frank "I wasn't talkin' abou' dinner. I was talkin' abou' the bleedin' sign. Anyhow, I bleedin' hate coddle, the slimy white sausages and the anaemic rashers floatin' in the potato juice is just disgustin'"

"Well it took you a long time to tell me that. You've been eatin' me coddle once a week for the forty years we've been married and ye' never opened yer gob before this. What's suddenly gor inta ya now?"

"Me mammy always told me Tha' it's nice ta be nice, an' I was always too embarrassed ta tell ya Tha I hated it till now. Since we're talkin' abou' it now, I might as well tell ya Tha I always gave it ta the moggie when yer back was turned, like" Frank looked suitably penitent at this astonishing confession.

"Well if tha's all the thanks I get after all these years" Josie riposted "Ye can make yer own bleedin' dinner in future" and she turned on her heel and stormed out

"Thank God" whispered Frank whilst the moggie looked downcast.

Civil Obedience

"Hello, what have we here?" Said the cop, opening the boot.

"It a bumpty bump"" said Freddie smiling guilelessly

"What'ddya mean?" Demanded the cop, not too impressed by Freddie's cheerful demeanour.

"Ah Officer, you're not too young to remember the song, you know, the one where the singer discovers a bumpty bump on the beach and spends the rest of his days trying to get rid of it. That's what this is"

With a thunderous frown the cop leaned menacingly into Freddie's window and snarled "OK smart arse, out of the car, right now. You need to modify your attitude when a Garda asks a civil question. You're off to the station with me and your car is impounded for a search for contraband items"

"Now officer Let's not be too hasty, you probably didn't recognise me in the car and all but I'm a person of considerable consequence. My name is Freddie Forsythe, I'm a famous writer and a fully paid up member of the Irish Diaspora. You really can't be dragging me off to the clink without a serious reason. Can't we be civil about all this. Why don't we start off all over again?"

"Listen" Rapped the cop, "if you don't shift yourself out of that car right now, I'll be forced to use my taser on you. I only got it last week and I haven't had an opportunity to use it since. You'd make an excellent first taste for it"

Freddie, nobody's fool, recognising that the situation had gotten out of hand opened the door and in doing so cracked the cop's knuckles which he had inadvertently left in an exposed position

He gazed in consternation as the cop writhed in agony clutching his injured knuckles in his other hand, issuing a stream of vituperation at Freddie and promising dire consequences whenever he had recovered enough to use his taser.

Freddie, nobody's fool, climbed back in the car and drove as rapidly as the speed limit would allow to the airport where he handed back the hired car and boarded his pre booked flight to the Bahamas. "I really hope his knuckles aren't broken" he mused.

Parenting

"What a child! we've reared a monster!" cried Tom.

"What's he done now?" Queried his long suffering wife June.

"He's thrown a brick through the Garda Superintendents front bedroom window, that's all" said Tom red in the face from either embarrassment or rage or both.

"But he's only three years old" wailed June "I know he's very strong for his age, but a brick through a bedroom window? how could he manage that?"

"Really" stormed Tom "That's all you have to say! How did he manage it? Have you any idea of the trouble we're in because of this carry on? Apparently, he also followed it up with a petunia in a flowerpot, just to add insult to injury like. I blame this on you, you have a right infantile delinquent made out of that boy. If this is his gig when he's three years old, what will he be like when he's a teenager?"

"He's just acting up, it's because you're never here. He doesn't have a proper male role model in his life. You're always either working late or down the pub with your darts mates. Don't blame me for this, wasn't your brother Jimmy sent to Borstal when he was a kid? I reckon he's taking after him"

"Ah that's a low blow. you know as well as I do that Jimmy was set up for that offence. That blackguard Fred Doyle from down the road led him astray and then ratted him out to the fuzz. Poor Jimmy got banged up for something he didn't do. Everybody knows that. Anyway, if you would let someone else babysit the brat maybe we could get a night out together sometime instead of hatching here all the time" Tom had always been a bit defensive about his brother's criminal conviction.

As they were discussing their problem child the doorbell rang.

Tom went to answer the doorbell and June heard a voice from the hall "Mr Brennan? We're from Child services"

Razorbill

"Where in the world has my pet razorbill gone? If someone's nicked my bird, I'll be very upset, and as everyone knows you wouldn't like me when I'm upset. Now, I want you all to form an orderly line over by the wall and I'll question each and every one of you in alphabetical order" Patrick, a man who was accustomed to getting his own way and didn't like being messed about, though he wasn't averse to messing others about, was in a raging temper

"Hang on a cotton pickin' minute here. I don't know who's ripped off your bleedin' avian or even if it's just taken it into its pointy head to feck off entirely of its own accord, but I've got more important things to be doing than hangin' around here whilst you subject innocent people to your version of an interrogation. I haven't had the pleasure of undergoing one of your question and answer sessions, but I wouldn't be surprised if it involved water boarding and sleep deprivation, so to hell with you and the bird you flew in on"

"See now that's just exactly the sort of response I'd expect from a gurrier like you. I've never been too enamoured by your joining our group and I wouldn't be surprised in the slightest if it was you that swiped my razorbill. It's just the sort of thing one of your type would think of doing just to upset me, and after all I've done for this group. I don't expect much in return, but simple civility would be nice when a person is put out like I am right now"

"Ah now, Patrick, there's no need to be calling names, Jimmy is no more a gurrier than you are an autocrat as he infers. I think we should all take a step back and draw a deep breath. Now when did you last see the errant fowl. Was he in his cage or flying around loose, someone might have left a window or door open and let him fly out? There's no cause to suspect fowl play here"

"It's a hen razorbill, anyone would know that if they knew anything about ornithology. And of course, she was in her cage, I don't let her loose around careless people when I'm out of the room, anyway she's very shy and she wouldn't leave her cage if I wasn't nearby"

With a loud screech and a flutter of wings the missing razorbill fluttered back into the room and with a triumphant coo she gulped down the sardine she had picked up somewhere "Jeez" she squawked "That's a horrible day out there, what's the craic folks? Anything good happen while I was out?"

Dreamtime

"Hold on to your dreams" Jimmy said in his usual condescending drawl.

"That's easy for you to say," Fiona Snarled "You haven't just gotten the property tax notice in the door for a dilapidated castle in the west of Ireland. You wouldn't believe the valuation those Pillocks in revenue have put on the mouldy pile of broken stones. I wouldn't grudge them the tax if the place was in habitable condition, at least I could rent it out to gullible Americans as my stately home"

"That's not a bad idea at all. Didn't you once tell me an unlikely story about someone or something haunting the place. The yanks would go ape for something like that. An ancestral castle and a genuine Irish ghost thrown in. They'd pay a fortune for the likes of that" Fiona could almost see the dollar signs lighting up Jimmy's eyes at the prospect of 'Money from America' as the old saying went.

"Your putting ideas in my head" Fiona mused "This is a ten pound castle, we could put the story of it in the advertising literature. And the hungry grass field just to the west of the castle"

"Hang on, hang on. What's all this ten pound castle and hungry grass stuff. I never heard of those things" Jimmy was seriously put out at the notion that someone knew something he didn't know. He was the epitome of the phrase Smart Alec.

"Jeez" laughed Fiona "I thought you knew everything. King Richard in the thirteenth century had a large surplus of underemployed younger sons of the nobility hanging around the palace of Westminster. He hit on this great scheme where he offered a grant of ten pounds to anyone of these layabouts who'd go to Ireland and build a castle. This had the double benefit of getting rid of the troublemakers and pacifying the uncouth native Irish into the bargain. A win, win situation for Richard and the Knights, not so much for the Paddies"

"The hungry Grass is a tale from the Great famine in Ireland when we lost three quarters of our population either through emigration or starvation. So great was the death toll that normal burial was impossible, so the dead were dumped in mass graves, without marker or record. Over the intervening years these mass graves have become indistinguishable from the surrounding countryside and unwary walkers who tread on such site will be struck by an unassailable hunger and they will fall down dead within seconds.

There are only two ways to avoid this fate. One is to always carry a crust of bread in your pocket and if you encounter the hungry grass you immediately start to chew on the crust, continuing to munch until you successfully navigate yourselves off the gravesite. The other method is to build up a layer of condition over your lifetime which will sustain you till you can traverse the cursed sod" He said, patting his ample paunch.

"And in your opinion" queried Jimmy "This will attract tourists?"

Bear Faced Cheek

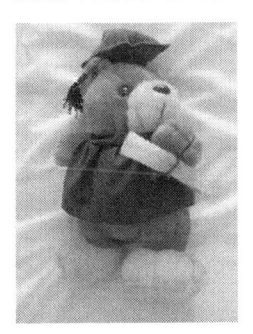

BA was wandering through the forest, clutching his recently awarded degree in Business Studies. Suddenly he was confronted by a vision of ursine loveliness, a fully formed and lustrous specimen of the bear tribe.

"What's your name Gorgeous? He queried, displaying his mortar board and certificate prominently. His mother had told him that the chicks fell for guys with degrees every time. And his mother had never lied in her entire sainted life, certainly not to BA anyway.

With a disgusted grunt the new love of his life turned and in typical bearish fashion shuffled off into the underbrush.

"What's with yer wan? BA asked himself "Is it possible that she's not bowled over by my clearly advertised erudition and scholarly diligence. Some people have no proper regard for the benefits of education"

"Hey, honeybear" he called loudly "wanna come play on the beach with me?" Receiving no reply, he headed down towards the beach musing, the while, on the fickleness of those of the feminine persuasion.

As he broke out of the trees, he found himself almost at the front door of a quaint, gingerbread style house. Finding himself hungry, as bears often do, he knocked on the door. Getting no response, he noticed that the door was ajar, so he pushed it open, shouting as he did so "Hello is anybody home?

BA Bear, Bachelor of Arts here. I just wondered if I could have a drink of water, maybe a crumb of a biscuit if there's one in the house?"

Getting no reply, he noticed that the house seemed to have a triune vibe going. Three chairs in varying sizes, three bowls of porridge in varying degrees of warmth and through an open door in the back a bedroom furnished in lavish style with three beds.

"Oh well, since there's no one her to eat this nice breakfast, I might as well help myself" and squeezing himself into the largest chair he polished off all three bowls of porridge, hot, cold and middling warm.

Being, as bears are wont to be, a little clumsy around the house, on rising from the chair he tipped it over onto the one beside it and that one into the littlest one, making kindling of all three.

"Oops" He muttered as he broke into a gigantic yawn "If I get to meet the owners, I must undertake to pay them back out of my first salary cheque, assuming that I get a job. Still I've got a degree in Management, I'm sure I'll get a well paid job in no time"

Feeling tired and emotional he stumbled into the bedroom and tripping over the smallest bed, smashing it in the process, he crashed headlong onto the other two and they suffered a similar fate

Rolling himself up in the bedding he murmured "I'll just close my eyes here for a couple of minutes. What can go wrong in a couple of minutes?"

Kidnapped

Tiger tiger burning bright

In the forest of the night

What immortal hand or eye

Could frame thy fearful symmetry.

William Blake

Really, I could have chosen a less dangerous victim for this caper. Millionaires children are ten a penny nowadays and you can trip over whiz kid entrepreneurs who've sold their start up company for multiple millions on every street corner.

So why, you might well ask, should I choose a Bengal Tiger for my hostage to fortune? It's quite simple really, when I was small my brother, thirteen years older than me and fully convinced before my arrival that he was destined to be the sole heir and apple of our parents' eye, bullied me unmercifully at every opportunity and none.

He took fiendish delight in frightening me whenever he could, mostly by setting traps and jumping out when least expected, sometimes late at night and dressed in fantastic costumes. He also told me horrifying stories, after we had been sent to bed in our pitch dark bedroom.

His favourite horror story involved a Bengal Tiger which was the feature of a circus. This monster beast, in his tale, invariably finished the story by devouring a small child, mostly a boy of tender years who had an older brother who rushed to the child's rescue and killed the animal but just too late to save the brother.

This tale haunted my dreams until well into adulthood and was responsible, according to my therapist for my recurring nightmares and chronic insomnia.

I was entranced to see a billboard advertising a circus coming to my neighbourhood last week. High on the list of attractions was Bernard the Bengal Tiger. I'm not sure what made me conceive the notion that here was my perfect opportunity to lay my ghosts to rest. My brother had died some years previously and I had never had the courage to confront him about his casual cruelty to my younger self, but surely this tiger was a gift from the gods to assuage my pain.

With the help of a tranquilliser gun and some dumb luck I managed to gain access to the Tigers cage late one moonless night. Having knocked the beast out I was confronted by the reality of the situation. Here I was with a half ton of sleeping savagery stretched in front of me and no thought out strategy for the next move.

My brothers voice resonated mockingly in my ears with his favourite catchphrase...

Be careful what you wish for!!

Clocks

Who winds up the clocks, and are they all in synch?

The German clock winder who came to Dublin, in the words of the old song, was up to no good, winding up a lot more than clocks, if the song is to be believed. Anyway, if he ever existed he would have been exhausted with his extramarital escapades and left with little energy to wind up the plethora of clocks in the picture.

A quick count of the timepieces in the picture gives a number somewhere above one hundred. If only one person was doing the winding and if each clock took one minute to wind the whole process would take an hour and forty minutes. To complicate the issue few of the clocks are equal in size or design and so it might be supposed that they were also unique in the winding key required to bring them to peak performance. Therefore, the time required for winding would need a fumble factor added to allow for the winder, the person who does the winding rather than the thing which he, or she uses, to accomplish the ideal tension. The time might easily be extended to two hours.

Now anyone with more than one clock under their control knows how difficult it is to keep them synchronised perfectly at the best of times. This process is even more complicated when the clocks in question are clockwork driven rather than electronic, or even atomic means. Hard as it may be to believe, even atomic clocks drift over time, calculated in centuries in the case of atomics.

All the above musing ran through Paddy's mind as he was ushered into the clock room as it was known. He had been overjoyed when he was contacted that morning with a job offer which called for two hours work each evening and a salary which was eye popping given the lenient hours involved. All he had to do was wind the clocks up and ensure that they all indicated the same time.

As he gazed in awe at the array of clocks in the room, he noticed a dishevelled individual crouched, mumbling, in the corner. Turning to his employer he asked who the man was and whether he was to remain there during Paddy's tour of duty.

"He's your predecessor" said his new boss "And it's your first duty to remove him from the room"

As Paddy bent to lift the unfortunate up, he heard him mumbling "I am an angry man, I vent in when I can, on the bag, not the skag"

Disappointment

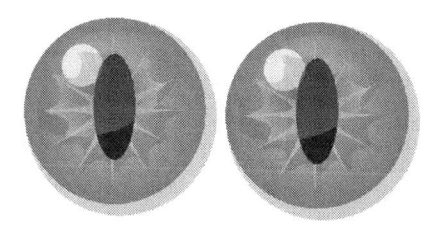

"Orange eyeballs?" Devin said "I've seen strange things before, but big Orange eyeballs suspended in midair in a darkened room is outside of my experience"

Advancing tentatively into the room and straining his eyes he said "Here kitty, kitty, nice kitty" why he had chosen to address the eyeballs as if they were belonging to a stray cat was not entirely clear to him but at least it had not provoked an instant attack.

As he stood wondering how to proceed a voice growled out of the darkness "Who the dickens do you think you're talking to in that idiotic singsong voice. You need to be quite a bit more respectful when addressing your moral and intellectual superiors" as the voice spoke the light in the room increased slowly to a point where Devin could just about make out an amorphous shape in the gloom.

"I'm very sorry if I've upset you but you must understand that in the dark, I could only see your eyes and with the vertical slit in the pupils I assumed you were some kind of cat. I can see now that I was wrong. Could we have a bit more light on the subject? I don't know about you, but my eyes don't work too well in this dim light"

"I see perfectly well in this or any light" said the other "I have no need to increase the light and there's no reason for me to improve your vision. You've been sent here as a meal for me. Now shut up and prepare to meet your doom" as the dim figure spoke Devin could just make out the gleam of the enormous fangs in his mouth and hear the snick of his claws as the extended out and scratched the floor between them.

"Now just a cotton picking minute here" Said Devin "We haven't even been introduced and here you are proposing to eat me. That's hardly civilised. Anyway, you could be in for a disappointment, I might make a difficult mouthful, even for a cat like creature such as yourself"

"If it's formality you want, I'm quite prepared to facilitate you. My name is (here he uttered a sound somewhere between a hiss and a squall) pleased to meet you, what's your name and can you be quick about it, it's fifteen years since I've eaten and I'm feeling a bit peckish"

"Just one moment" Replied Devin as he entered the adjacent phone box in the corner of the room and spun around to emerge in a blue long sleeved tee shirt, red underpants and leather knee high boots.

"In the light of this new development" said the catlike one "I'd like to renegotiate" and with a loud hiss he disappeared in a puff of blue smoke.

Don't Open It!

"Who died and made you the boss?" Demanded Allison "I found it so I'm keeping it, so there"

"That's just not fair" whined Dierdre "Somebody lost that and they're probably crying their eyes out about it right now. You know as well as I do that it's not something you'd like to lose yourself"

"Well finders keepers" snapped Allison "All I know is that you just want to get your hands on it for yourself. You were always a covetous little snot and you don't fool me. I've known you all your life, after all"

As the verbal temperature rose and the girls faced off, the lid of the brass bound, oak, chest which they had happened upon began to rise with a creepy groaning noise.

Allison, who was facing towards the box released a piercing scream and with her normally well groomed hair standing out in a halo around her head gazed in open mouthed horror at the apparition which was snaking its nebulous way out into the room.

"What are you yelling about?" Demanded Dierdre "You're such a drama queen, if it means that much to you, you can keep the bloody box" she had not noticed the scene unfolding behind her. She got, however, a rude awakening as she found herself being dragged by her hair towards the box.

Faced by the frightful apparition with its ephemeral appearance, gaping jaws and long, curved fangs she fainted dead away.

Seeing her sister being dragged towards a terrible fate, Allison burst into frantic activity. She grabbed Deirdre's ankles and pulling with superhuman strength provided by her panic state she managed to dislodge the spectre's grip on her.

Inspired by the many horror movies she remembered from her younger days she grabbed two wooden spoons off the kitchen table where she and Dierdre had been standing and forming them into a crude wooden cross she confronted the apparition "I abjure thee in the name of the father, the son and the Holy Ghost" She intoned in what she hoped was the proper tone of voice, advancing as she spoke.

The spectre took one disbelieving look at her and opening its cavernous mouth swallowed Allison, Dierdre and a significant portion of the kitchen furniture in one gulp.

With a loud belch he said: "That's lunch sorted, I wonder what's for dinner" and he crawled, sluggishly back into his box.

Traffic Chaos

Leaping balletically from the top deck of the bus Seamus called out 'Watch out below, superhero coming down."

Derry Dolphin, passing by and minding his own business felt the brunt of Seamus's size sixteen boots on the point of his nose.

"What the hell do you think you're doing?" He squeaked in fluent Dolphin, or maybe not so fluent Dolphin since his nose was bent severely out of shape.

"Very sorry". Replied Seamus as he brushed Dolphin snot off his shiny superhero boots. "I'm a member of the National League of Superheroes, I'll thank you to stand, or swim out of my way. I have had a call from headquarters to attend to some superhero type business. Time Is of the essence here so, if you would release your grip on my cape, I'd appreciate it"

Since Derry showed no inclination to release his bite on Seamus's cloak, he gave a sharp yank and only succeeded in tearing a large lump out of his splendid apparel.

"Now look what you've done, you awkward bloody cetacean" snarled a, by now, seriously upset Seamus "That was my very best superhero cape and I have a date later in the evening with Marvellous Mary, the Titaness of Thunder, she's very hot and if there's one thing she likes in her dates and that's that they should look cool you've ruined everything, you cretin"

"Hey now" Protested Derry "I was just passing by, minding my own business and you fell down on top of me with your oversized boots and your bad attitude. I'm the aggrieved party here. I held onto your idiotic cape to stop you from rushing off without exchanging insurance details. We are a civilised society, are we not?"

"Don't try to wriggle your way out of this you smelly old fish you. Just exactly what did you think you were doing overtaking a bus on the left hand side. Don't you know that swimmers must always pass on the right. Have you never read the rules of the road? Now get out of my way before I'm forced to get rough with you"

Doggone

"Juno's gone'" Cried Abigail, tears streaming down her parchment white face "Someone has stolen her. She was here just a moment ago.

"Not a very likely story" thought James Busteed, prominent member of the independent Republic of Cork. "She most likely let the blasted animal stray again. It's extraordinary how often when people say something was there just a moment ago it actually subsequently turned out that it was anything but just a moment, in fact, quite often significant periods of time may have passed by. Still I suppose we'll have to do something about the mangy bitch. Juno, I mean, not Abigail"

Abigail meanwhile was fluttering up and down the strand calling out in a piteous whine interspersed with racking sobs "here Juno, here girl"

"James" She sobbed "What are we going to do? I'm convinced that someone has stolen our darling Juno. We must report her loss to the police. I'm sure they'll be interested in a case of dog napping, won't they? I know why don't we swim out to the cave over there and see if she's there, it's an easy swim and we can quickly be back here if she turns up here

Assuming his most magisterial air James said in his irritating tone of voice "We'll do that immediately and the we'll go to the office of Cork Advertiser and Commercial Register and place an advertisement in its lost and found column. I'm sure they'll give it a prominent position in the paper, I'm a close friend of the editors you know"

"Oh James, would you. I was under the impression that you didn't like my Juno. That's why I refused your kind offer of marriage last week. I couldn't live with someone who doesn't adore my beautiful canine friend"

"My darling Abigail" James protested fulsomely "Of course I like your dog, perhaps not sitting up and eating off the dinner table with us, but in her proper place, the outside kennel perhaps"

"James" Said Abigail sternly "Methinks you doth protest too much. I detect a distinct coolness in your demeanour when you talk about my darling pet. I'm beginning to harbour suspicions that you might have some part in her mysterious disappearance. Is it possible that it's all a dastardly plot to separate me from Juno?"

With a sly smile James said "Darling girl, you're stressed out about your poor dog, only that could explain your hurtful accusations. I think I should bring you to the Chinese Restaurant for dinner. You're probably hungry and I believe they have a new dish of the day on the menu tonight"

Dream killer

"I never signed up for this crap" cried Samantha "I was a talented writer and painter with a fabulous social life and all the world at my feet, next thing I meet that rat James and before you can say Jack Robinson I'm up to my oxters in smelly nappies, potato peelings and squalling kids. Where did it all go wrong"

As she stood there in her shabby kitchen a voice spoke "You know" it said "You don't have to put up with all this. Play your cards right and you could be down in the Caribbean on a fantastic yacht drinking mimosas with the Kardashians"

"Who said that" Samantha gasped frantically scanning for the source of the voice.

"Down here" replied the scruffy teddy bear lying discarded in the corner of the room.

"It's finally gotten to me" She sobbed "I've lost my marbles, talking teddy bears, they'll be sending for the men in the white coats next"

"Cool your jets missus" the bear replied "You haven't fallen off your mental perch. It's actually me that's talking to you. I'm really your fairy godfather. The original winged little man persona has been outdated for the past few years due to rebranding issues in fairyland and they've stuck me with this ludicrous get up, bloody marketing people uh?"

"Anyway, amongst other trials they've stuck me with is that I can't walk. I can talk alright, and I have the ability to grant the customary three wishes. Thank God they haven't messed with that gift, otherwise there wouldn't be much need for fairy godfathers, now would there?"

"So, let's not rush into anything, but would you like to give some thought to the three wishes caper? It's not that I'm in a hurry, you understand, but I do have a number of clients and the guys on the top floor expect that we grunts will get through a certain number of calls in the day. The bastards have cut our wages recently too and the latest rumour is that they're going to outsource the fairy godfather gig to Korea or Pakistan"

Samantha was completely overwhelmed "Three wishes?" She asked "What sort of wishes, does it have to be something like world peace or elimination of poverty or hunger or something like that? Truth is, I'd really like a washing machine that works, this bloody thing is broken down more often than it is working. But what would James say? I think I'll have to wait till he comes home. I don't feel comfortable making decisions on my own, you see"

"Ah jaysus missus, will you wake up and get a grip" snapped the FG "You're a grown adult woman for God's sake. You don't need a man to approve your decisions, these wishes are for you, not for that drunken ne'er do well husband. If I was you, my first wish would be to banish him to a desert island, preferably somewhere inside the Arctic circle"

Broccoli House.

Paddy was, to say the least, quite confused. He was standing one minute on O'Connell Street minding his own business when suddenly everything went black, just for a second. Next thing he knew he was confronted by a completely different scene.

The spire lay, a twisted wreck sprawled on top of the smouldering remains of the GPO and Clerys was a pile of shattered masonry while all around the scene of devastation continued as far as the eye could see.

As he stood there mouth agape a man came scurrying by. "You best shut yer trap and get in outta the sun, mister" the passerby said in a hoarse whisper.

"What's going on" pleaded Paddy. "What happened?"

"Ah no, not another one" moaned the man "You're one of them time travellers, aren't you? You just appeared here outta nowhere didn't you? Come with me. We need to get under cover, or they'll snatch us up"

Grabbing Paddy by the arm he dragged him down the devastated Talbot street and dodged into the shattered remains of Guiney's store. Paddy found himself being dragged headlong down to the Stygian depths of the basement level.

"What's going on" He demanded.

305

"Shh" cautioned his companion "You need to be very quiet; they have very keen hearing you know"

Digging his heels in Paddy snarled "No I don't know; I don't know anything. Where are we and who are "they" when they're at home?"

"It's the Leprechauns don't you know. They've risen up and taken over. They live above ground now in little tree houses built on florets of broccoli. They don't have any use for us big people, so they hunt us for the craic. If they catch us, they skin us and use our pelts for clothing. Apparently, the height of fashion for their little women is a human skin coat, preferably draped to ground level. It doesn't have to be a very big human skin as their women are really, really, small"

"Back in the year 2015 they got sick and tired of lurking about underground and worrying about their crocks of Gold. Apparently, they had to keep moving them every couple of weeks because the developers were digging up every acre of land to build more useless monstrosities, so the little people rose up and whacked the whole lot of us. That's when the time slips started"

As he spoke there was a scratching noise and a spark lit up his grimy face. "There's only one thing we can do" he said, handing Paddy a large screw like device "This Is an awl" he said "We need to dig a tunnel and delve ourselves deep underground it's quite simple really"

"An awl" said a puzzled Paddy "What's an awl?"

Travelling Hazards

Having carefully prepared everything in advance, packed with weight limits in mind and the likelihood of needing formal clothing we arrived at the check in desk full to the brim with vim and vinegar.

"Passports please" Said the attractive lady at the check-in desk.

"Certainly" I replied insouciantly.

"Sorry Sir" She said, looking not sorry in the least "These passports are out of date"

"Oh bugger" I said "What happens now?"

"Well, you need up to date passports and the only place you'll get them is the Department of Foreign Affairs in Stephens Green. The passport office is closed on Saturdays. Unfortunately, you will miss your flight. You couldn't make it into town and back in time"

"I'll call Sarah Jane and she'll come back and bring us into town" Said She Who Must Be Obeyed "We'll need to get photos done and nip down to the cop shop to get them stamped and we should have them done by the time she gets back to pick us up"

After a mad scramble to get the photos and a hair raising ride into Stephens Green we arrived at the Department of Foreign Affairs.

There followed an agonisingly long procedure culminating finally with the issuing of temporary passports.

Sarah Jane had remained, parked illegally outside waiting to take us back to the airport.

Image my surprise when, on the security camera in the concierge's office I saw a police car drawing up to the back of her car. More astoundingly the driver of the bipsy got out and going to the boot of Sarah's car, commenced to take our luggage out and transfer it to his boot.

She who etc. now returned from the office where she had been picking up the passports and said "Come on, we might make it back in time to catch the flight"

"What's going on" I pleaded

"It's my squash partner Frank" She replied "He was on duty today and I gave him a call. He's bringing us to the Airport"

In my experience, there's no better way to get to the airport than in the back of a police car, despite what my friend might think.

Arachnophobia

> Little Miss Muffet,
> Sat on her tuffet,
> Eating some curds and whey,
> Along came a spider,
> Who sat down beside her,
> And frightened Miss Muffet away.

"Ah" sighed Miss Muffet known to an intimate circle of friends and relatives as Jemima "there's nothing quite like a nice bowl of curds and whey for breakfast"

Her Father, Abercrombie, looked with some disgust at her choice of food and continued to snarf down his full Irish breakfast.

"I don't know how you can face that stuff in the cold light of morning" he said disparagingly.

"You just have no appreciation of the finer things of life" replied Jemima "This is chock full of antioxidants, vitamins and other good things which I can't think of right now" and she carried on stuffing her gub with the aforesaid gloop.

Suddenly Jemima let out a piercing scream and jumped up on the table, scattering the breakfast dishes and, sadly her Father's full Irish, which he had been enjoying enormously.

"What in God's name is the matter with you?" Demanded Abercrombie who had been carefully minding his last, Superquinn, sausage. He was particularly fond of Superquinn sausages and always reserved one as a polisher offer at breakfast. Now he watched in dismay as Bonzo, the schitsu greedily gobbled the tasty morsel.

"The, the, the Spider" Screeched Jemima "It's as big as my head" and she pointed to an, admittedly large, though hardly head sized arachnid dangling from the light fitting. "Do something Father. I am deathly afraid of spiders and that monster looks bloated on someone's blood"

As Abercrombie struggled to raise his rotund bulk from his chair the spider spoke "It's not very nice to comment on someone's size" He snapped "You're a bit large in the arse yourself. Please give over the histrionics, settle down and I'll tell you guys a sad story"

Just as Seraphim, for that was the spider's name, was about to launch into his tale, James the butler arrived to check if everything was all right for the diners.

"I'm extremely sorry about that Miss Muffet" he tended to be a bit formal in his speech, "The new housemaid evidently did not dust the breakfast room adequately.

"It's not the first time she's shirked her duties I'm afraid. She'll just have to go, Miss" and taking up the silver cover which had been used to keep the Full Irish warm on its long journey from the subterranean kitchen he bashed Seraphim, swept his corpse into the upturned cover and calmly exited the room.

Cruella de Ville

"Spelunking?" She cried incredulously "Are you out of your freaking mind? That's scrambling around in dark, damp, smelly and insanitary caves isn't it? This is the famous big surprise you planned for our first month's anniversary. Have you noticed what I'm wearing? A light top, short skirt and six inch stiletto heels. When was the last time you saw someone dressed like this in a freaking cave, for God's sake"

"Take it easy, I've packed appropriate gear for the trip. It would hardly be a surprise if I'd told you what to wear beforehand, now would it?" he temporised, thinking that perhaps this was not the brightest idea in the bright ideas box.

"Listen you gobshite, there's no way in hell I'm going down a dark hole in the ground with you or anybody else, appropriate gear or not. Now, tell me, when's the next bus out of here back to civilisation. I'll leave you to your spelunking and I'll celebrate the end of our relationship in Coppers this evening, hopefully I'll meet someone who's not into dank, cold and creepy places. By the way, don't call me and I won't call you, OK?"

He pondered the intricacies of the female mind as he rappelled down into the cave on his own, ignoring the first rule in the spelunker's handbook namely, never go down in the caves on your own, even if you're an experienced caver.

"What's wrong with her anyway" he thought "Caves are beautiful, look at all the beautiful stalactites and stalagmites, glistening in the light from my headlamp, and the multiple colours in the stone, it's like a fairyland. If she had given it a chance, she'd have been stunned I'm sure"

Finally, after a considerable time underground, tired but satisfied, he turned to retrace his steps. As he got to the point where his rope led upwards at a steep angle, he found that it was lying in a coil on the floor of the cave.

Looking at the end of the rope he saw that it had been roughly hacked through and thrown down the tunnel, leaving him with no way to climb out.

Crying out in despair he shouted "That bitch, she really does reap a cruel revenge"

Bravery or Temerity?

"I think I'll go for a swim" said the girl in the blue bikini.

"Are you out of your mind?" I demanded "Have you seen the size of the breakers out there. People have been sucked out to sea and never seen again all along this coast, some of them not even meaning to go in the water. Get a grip girl, there's perfectly safe swimming just two hundred metres down the coast"

"What made you so wise and your mother so foolish" she riposted with an impish smile as she performed a perfect swallow dive and disappeared under the waves.

She reappeared some fifty metres out from her entry point and waved frantically as a vortex formed around her and dragged her out of sight. As she fell from sight, I heard her despairing cry "It's a portal, nobody told me there were portals around here"

I'm not entirely sure If it was derring do or curiosity that drove me but without thinking I dived in after her.

Reaching out at my fullest extent I felt the briefest touch of her fingers, but I could not maintain my grip. The vortex which took her rejected me and a moment later I found myself thrown unceremoniously on the rocks.

Later, in the pub I related my tale to a spellbound audience of tourists, locals and an ancient fisherman.

"Ah, that's Castle Cove, that is" Said the ancient "Around here we avoid Castle Cove. Everyone knows that the Pookahs live in the water surrounding those parts and each year they take a mortal, usually a good looking girl and drag them down to their submarine depths. Many's the unwise lassie whose last glimpse of the surface world was Castle Cove"

"So, if that's the thing" I demanded "Why didn't they take me along with her, I was at the edge of the vortex after all, they could just as easily have had two as one. This whole story sounds inherently unlikely"

"I have it on the best of authority" replied the odoriferous angler "Sure didn't James Joyce himself say 'A man's errors are the portals of his discovery' and don't we live in an era of sexual equality nowadays so if women want to tempt the Pookahs then they must suffer the consequences. That James Joyce knew a thing or two, so he did"

Performance Anxiety

The Auld Triangle

"Jaysus, it's bleedin cold here" Freddy said, teeth chattering as he clung to the pitching door in the stormy ocean "how did I get here in the first place? Last I knew I was waiting in line to be interviewed for the X Factor. If this is some sort of trick that Simon Cowell is in for a good kicking when I get him"

As the storm abated somewhat, he found a key card clenched in his teeth. "What's this for" He muttered. "It hardly works on anything out here in the middle of the sea. Might as well try it on this door since there certainly is nowhere else for miles around" and he slid the card into the door lock. Hardly had he done so than the door swung open inwards, catapulting him into the room inside.

As he sprawled on the deep pile carpet in the room, he heard the door slam behind him and he scrambled onto his feet, assuming a martial arts pose which he had seen on television. He immediately felt foolish as there was nobody in the room except himself and no obvious dangers either, not at he could have dealt with dangers as he was a card carrying coward at the best of times.

Suddenly the end wall of the room rose into the ceiling and he found himself in the wings of an enormous stage with the X Factor judges lined up in front of the auditorium. On stage there was a lady doing something unusual with a flock of pigeons and a sealed packet of birdseed. As she came to the end of her performance there was a huge burst of applause from an invisible audience.

As Freddy stood wondering if he was dreaming a loud voice called "And our next act is Freddy Fortescue who will demonstrate his amazing flexible rubber man skills"

As he had entered the competition as a ballad singer Freddy was understandably confused by this rubber man thing. On top of that cause of confusion he was stark naked as the day he was born and given the volume of applause for the pigeon lady there was obviously quite a large audience in the venue. All things considered Freddy decided that he was not ready to perform in public just yet.

He was not given any option however as the flat behind him started to move slowly but inexorably into the stage area, pushing him forcibly onto the centre spot however unwilling he might be.

"Oh, what the hell" He thought and to thunderous applause he opened his mouth and gave a rousing rendition of "The Auld Triangle"

Childhoods End

I grew up in the shadow of Croke Park and spent what can reasonably be termed an idyllic childhood there.

Games of hopscotch, called beds in my day were common for girls, boys would rather die than be seen hopping from square to square kicking a polish tin full of gravel before them.

Boys games were of a somewhat more rambunctious type, we had Relievio, which entailed one person closing his eyes and counting to one hundred whilst the others ran away and concealed themselves in the gardens around about. When the count was over the counter then attempted to capture the concealed. Sadly, for him when he had managed to capture some of his victims another one of the concealed would run out from behind him and relieve the captured. I don't think a game of Relievio ever ended with all the escapers rounded up.

Another favourite was boxing the fox, or to give it its proper name robbing orchards. This entailed waiting till after dark, usually in late autumn and climbing over the walls of those fortunate enough to have fruit trees in their back gardens. Depending on whose orchard we raided the spoils were better or worse but the penalties for being caught ranged from a clout around the head to a caning and, if a miscreant was caught in an orchard belonging to someone of the higher orders like the

Archbishop of Dublin or the retired Judge Gough, then court and a fine, or worse was likely.

Funnily enough I cannot remember eating any of the stolen fruit as it tended to be underripe when the raids took place and consequently ended up being kicked along the roads on our way home.

My best friend at the age of twelve and thirteen was a lad called Aloysius Kennedy who lived directly across the road from me. He and I were nearly the same age and had similar interests.

We were fond of a game which entailed carefully avoiding walking on cracks in the pavement when walking out. If you accidentally stepped on a crack your companion would cry out "Harry kissed the Devil" this was considered a bad thing.

One damp spring morning Alo and me were heading off to school and I proposed a game of Kiss the Devil. Alo replied "That's a kid's game" in a dismissive tone of voice. Looking back through the tunnel of the long years I reckon that that was the first moment when I realised, I was no longer a child.

A New Beginning

"What in the name of all that's good and holy is that" Demanded Jimmy staring in astonishment at the strange flying machine approaching at an insane pace.

Clutching her gin and tonic tightly Mary blanched and said "I'm afraid it's coming for me, darling. There's something I should have told you before about my earlier life. You see I'm not from around here, in fact I'm from very, very, far away from here. The binary star system Epsilon Eridani actually. I figure my Dad has Sussed out where I've been for the past twenty years and has sent his goons to pick me up"

"But, but, but" Stammered Jimmy with his mouth agape.

"Please darling" Mary pleaded "Close your mouth, it's very unattractive with your tonsils visible. And please stop with the stammering. My Dad won't be one bit impressed with a stammering imbecile when we go to meet him"

"Now just a cotton picking minute" Jimmy snapped "What's all this about going to meet your Dad. This is the first I've heard of any relations of yours" He spoke in a rising voice as the Craft was now hovering over their hotel balcony and the noise of its motor was becoming deafening

"Well this is just a bit embarrassing" Mary cooed "My Dad is the Lord High Pooh Bah of the Epsilon Eridani System which has two Suns and twenty seven inhabited planets. Some years ago, I got a bit fed up with all the fuss and bother of being his only daughter and I upped and fled to Earth for a new beginning. I thought I'd covered my tracks very well but obviously with the resources of two suns and twenty seven planets at his command I suppose it was inevitable he'd catch up on me sometime. I guess I miscalculated"

Above them a triangular opening was irising in the base of the flying machine and Jimmy could see three strange looking, six armed creatures, with various sharp implements clutched in their claws gazing down at him with anything but friendly intentions on their faces.

"These are the goons, I suppose" He muttered "I hope you can talk to them because I don't see them as being very friendly"

"Actually, I'm alright, being a princess of noble blood and all but your position is a bit dicey" Replied Mary "They've probably been told to bring me back unharmed but anyone else is likely to be sliced and diced. I'm terribly sorry about this but I'm sure you understand, don't you dear. this isn't you dear, it's me, don't you know"

Patrick Puffin

"What exactly does that mean? The wind is never weary" demanded Patrick Puffin through a mouthful of sardines.

Sarah Seagull sternly took him to task "didn't your mother ever tell you that it's rude to talk with your mouth full. Nobody wants to be looking into your open beak when they're having a conversation with you. Now please finish what you're eating and start again"

Gulping down the offending fishes Patrick retorted "Who died and made you mistress of the universe and arbiter of all things etiquette? If I want to talk with my beak full I will, and no stuck up amphibian dive bomber is going to dictate to me"

"Now, now children" chided Desmond the Double Crested Cormorant in a sonorous voice in keeping with his grand sounding title, quite out of keeping with his rather drab plumage, which was in his out of breeding season rather dull blackish brown colouring

"Surely there's no need for this type of antagonism amongst fellow seabirds. After all is said and done, we're all fishing in the same ocean, aren't we? You should know by now Sarah, that poor Patrick is a victim of his genetic heritage as are we all and speaking with a full mouth is a natural for him as preying on lesser creatures is for one of your family. And Patrick, your response to Sarah is unnecessarily harsh. She is one of the alpha predators of our little community and she feels a somewhat natural entitlement to stick her beak in where it's not asked for, she's no more responsible for her behaviour than you are"

"Will you guys please knock off with the whinging and quarrelling" Demanded Albert the Albatross "If you'd been condemned to hang around the neck of the Ancient Mariner for all eternity, you'd have something to moan about. He deserved to suffer for his carry on, but what'd I do to be stuck, dangling, head down for the rest of time?"

Jerking her head Sarah said "Not that old Ancient Mariner song and dance again. Patrick, I've heard this tune too many times, what say we go hunting fish for a while, the wind is never weary, and we can coast on its broad back for ages without having to listen to misery guts here?"

Bucking Bronco

"We must kill him" said Cuddles the kitten "He knows too much"

Unbeknownst to the adorable pair Barney the Bucking Bronco was eavesdropping outside the door and was fully aware of their dastardly plotting.

"If they think they're going to off me as easy as that they have another think coming" He swore.

Quietly he stole away to the stables where his bucking outfit was waiting for his next gig as "Barney the Buckingest Bronco this side of the Old West"

Shrugging into his hand made costume he grumbled to himself "You just can't please some people. I've dedicated my whole life to this travelling Wild West show, from Colt to stallion and all I get by way of recompense is a conspiracy to have me topped. And by a pair of tiny fur balls to boot. What is it I'm supposed to know anyway? Everybody knows I've a head like the proverbial broken sieve and if ever I fell on a secret, I'd have forgotten it within fifteen seconds. Attention span of the average goldfish me"

Meanwhile back in the main house the kittens were discussing the best method for removing Barney without implicating themselves. "I think we should poison his feed" said cuddles. "We're so lovable nobody would ever suspect us"

"That's easier said than done" Replied Tickles "Where would we get the poison, and how much of it would we need, he's a big horse after all. Do you even know what's poisonous for horses anyway?"

"Oh, don't be always so negative. This is a horse farm isn't it. There's no end of stuff we could give him lying around, besides there's ragwort growing in the back field, we could get a big bunch of that and mix it with his feed, he's so dopey he'd never notice until he's lying on his back with his legs in the air"

"Don't you think somebody would notice if they found us harvesting ragwort? It's no exactly normal behaviour for little balls of adorableness you know. No, we need to be a bit more creative. I favour him having an accident, horses are always falling and breaking their necks and bucking Broncos must be especially prone to accidents. It's a high risk career after all"

As he described Barney's downfall Tickles drew imaginary pictures in the air, pausing to tangle the ball of wool she had stolen from the woman of the houses basket.

Totally engrossed in their nefarious plotting they failed to see Barney approaching on tippy toes, not an easy thing for a horse to accomplish, but Barney was a consummate showbiz animal.

The first that the kittens knew of Barney's presence was when he went into his bucking bronco routine, leaping and stamping in a violent frenzy. The pair were tossed willy nilly back and forth beneath his flashing hooves, escaping their doom by the skin of their teeth.

Finally, they managing to escape through a partially open window and fleeing from the house Cuddles was heard to say, "Showbiz is not the only career you know, let's find something less perilous OK?

Book Burning

"Throw another one of them books on the fire" Cried Billy "They really make the nicest of blazes"

James looked troubled "It's a bit sacrilegious burning books, isn't it? I mean anyone in history who practised it was considered a bit off. I'm thinking of the Nazis and good old Savonarola, who came to a sticky end, having made his name for book burning, amongst other things"

Sarah took a deep breath and said to James "I normally defer to your opinions, James, you being my boss and all, but I this case I think you're wrong. As far as I can see there's an avalanche of rubbishy books being published these days since Amazon and CreateSpace came on the scene and, with some shining exceptions, the best thing that could be done with them is to throw them behind the fire. There they would at least be an environmentally sound contribution to the global warming thing. I mean, burnt bullshit has to be good for warming the globe, no?"

Picking up a copy of the latest self published masterpiece Billy hurled it onto the flames and said "Reading is for wimps. Why read at all nowadays. We've come a long way since what's his name invented the printing press. We've got television, the Internet, smart phones, Twitter, snapchat, old uncle Cobley and all. so why waste time and energy on reading, it's just a waste of paper and ink, if you ask me"

"Nobody asked you" Snarled James as he set fire to Billy's wheelchair "See how you like a taste of your own medicine" and turning to Sarah he said, "Haven't you got some filing or typing or something to be doing?

Prompt Prompts

"The happiness of your life depends on the quality of your thoughts - Marcus Aurelius"

Who is this Marcus Aurelius gink anyway? and what qualifies him to pontificate to us on an irregular basis whenever he feels the urge to pop his head out of the prompts bag?

I've a strong suspicion that he was deeply into the poppy fields himself. He'd have been quite happy thinking or not thinking either way, if that suspicion is accurate.

Some say he was a Roman Emperor but was that something to brag about? he had to put his trousers on one leg at a time like all the rest of us.

What's that I hear some of you say? He was a Roman and they didn't wear trousers? that's just ridiculous. the draught around his nether regions would have been unbearable. It might have been ok in a Roman summer but in winter Rome can be quite chilly, so I'm told.

Anyway, knickerless or otherwise it turns out that he couldn't even hack the emperor gig by himself, he had to have a co-emperor, first his daddy and after he popped his clogs Marcus's son stepped into the breach.

Modern dictators seem to have the good grace to wait til their predecessor has shuffled off the mortal coil before they jump in.

Look at Kim Jung Un for instance, he seems to manage quite well without needing an elderly relative, or a compliant son, to lean on. In point of fact, being an elderly relative of the bould Kim is a tricky position to hold if his uncle and older brother were anything to go by.

So down with Marcus Aurelius, I say. We should find someone more uplifting and agreeable to provide us with prompts in future.

How about Michael Healey Ray?

Laced Up

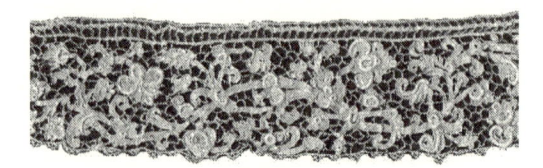

It was extraordinary how he could feel so full of confidence, given that he was as thick as two short planks, ugly as sin and suffered from chronic halitosis.

Still his mother had always told him that confidence comes from within and his one shining characteristic was that he'd always paid attention to what his mother said.

On this Thursday morning as he dressed himself in his interview suit, he needed all the reassurance he could muster since he was heading off to catch the bus to meet his prospective new employer.

Trotting down the stairs from his dingy bed sit on the South Circular Road he almost tripped over a slip of lace which had found its way onto the middle step.

Reaching down without pausing, he picked up the offending obstacle and noticed it was uniquely beautiful.

"That looks like a lucky charm" he muttered to himself as he went towards the front door.

Suddenly there was a flash of pinkish light and he was confronted by an apparition of an amazing lady, dressed in a long flowing lace dress.

"That's mine" she said in a musical voice, pointing towards his pocket where he had thrust the slip of lace.

"What do you mean? What's yours" queried our hero, completely forgetting that he had picked up the lace slip.

"The slip of lace" snapped the lady, obviously not impressed by his obtuseness

"Oh that, no problem, here it is, I'm very glad to reunite you with it, it's very lovely and it deserves to rejoin the rest of the dress"

Instantly mellowing the lady said "thank you, that's very good of you. That piece of lace is very valuable to me. Without it I couldn't do my magic, I'd be royally screwed. I have an appointment with Cinderella later and, god knows, she needs all the magic she can get. Is there anything I can do for you in the magic line to express my gratitude?"

"Well I have this big interview later and I could probably do with a bit of help in it" he said, hopefully

She looked at him with her big blue eyes and said "Sorry, son, I'm magic, not miraculous" and with another flash of pinkish light she disappeared.

Hyacinths and Roses

Lurking in the recesses of the hyacinth and rose filled secret garden lives the hobgoblin King, Ferdia.

Ferdia is a rather nasty and pugnacious King, unlike many of his fellow monarchs, so anyone who visits his hideaway stands an excellent chance of being stung to death by his regiment of giant African Killer bees.

It might seem to be a bit over the top for him to employ a full regiment of the aforementioned African Killer Bees but his is a heredity position and as everybody knows, heredity doesn't count for much nowadays. In fact, Ferdia had just last week survived his twelfth assignation attempt. So prevalent had these attacks on his August person become that he had recently changed the family motto from the poncy Latin "Ars Gratia Artis" so familiar to movie goers of a certain generation, to the more appropriate "Just Because You're Paranoid Doesn't Mean They Are Not All Out To Get You" This motto was now emblazoned, at great expense, on all points of prominence throughout the extent of Ferdia's realm.

On the other side of the bay stands the Sugar Loaf mountain, looming over the southern aspect of the countryside and presided over by The grand Panjarandum Leo The Magnificent, a vertically challenged, four foot high little man with enormous delusions of grandeur.

Leo had just that morning been informed by one of his legion of informers of Ferdia's change of status and was in a state of furious rage and frustration.

"Who does this jumped up pillock think he is" He roared, his rage so incandescent that a huge smoke ring issued from his head and hovered menacingly over the Mountain.

"So, he has a regiment of African Killer Bees, does he, well I'll show him" And turning to his necromancer who was, as always, standing close by he ordered "Prepare me a potion which will disable or kill these pernicious flying assassins and order my fighting battalions of fire Ants to gird themselves for battle"

The ensuing war is set fair to go down in history as the longest and most devastating ever witnessed in the history of the world.

Tune in next week for instalment two of the battle of Booterstown.

Plain Sailing

When I pulled over to change the tyre, I was surprised to find that the thumping noise was coming from the boot. I was quite certain that I had given him enough happy juice to keep him quiet until we had reached our destination.

So, I grabbed the socket wrench and dashed around to the back of the car, whipped open the boot and administered a sharp tap to the top of his head, just as it emerged groggily out of the darkness.

"That should keep you safe and snug until we get there" I said and closed down the lid, just in time as I was lit up by the lights of a cop car approaching.

"Are you OK?" Queried the portly officer, through the open window, from the comfort of his driving seat

"Yeah, no problem" I replied "Just finished. I'll just check that the nuts are tight and then I'll be off"

"OK so" He grunted and buzzing up the window he headed off in the direction of town.

Fifteen minutes later I rolled into Howth sailing club, hoping that there would be nobody around. As it happened, the night was ideal for my purposes, with a howling gale blowing sleet and rain horizontally into my face.

Dashing around to the boot I bundled him into a large duffel bag which I had brought for the purpose and loaded him onto a nearby trolley. I then headed through the gate and down the slip to my boat, "The Lazy Daze"

Just as I got to my craft a voice hailed me "Hey Danny, what in God's name are you doing out on a night like this. I hope you're not thinking of going out on the wild sea in this weather?"

It was Jim Bennett, the secretary and head Nosy Parker of our sailing club.

"No Jim" I replied "I'm just getting set up for the regatta on Tuesday, best to be prepared, don't you know"

Well aware that my suggestion would be rejected I said; "Would you like to give me a hand with this duffel?"

"Ah no, sorry, bad back you know. Old war wound"

Highly relieved I said "No problem Jim, I'll manage"

As he turned to retrace his steps to the comfort of the members bar, I thought to myself "That was too close for comfort. Why can't you keep your trap shut Danny?"

Oh lucky Man

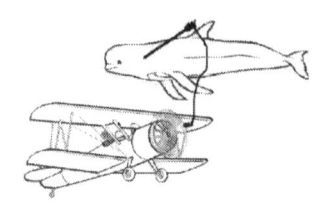

"This whole situation is inherently unlikely, if not totally impossible" Peter gazed upwards at the blimp sized whale which had become entangled in his World War One antique flying machine

"Never mind how unlikely it is" snapped his lady wife who was known, far and wide, for her command of the bitter word "How do you propose to get us out of this 'situation' as you call it. I told you at the get go that flying around in this orange box was a sure way to get us killed, but did you listen? did you ever. Now I would strongly urge you to get your arse in gear and disconnect us from your piscatorial friend up there before he decides to dive back down into his natural element. I don't fancy swimming home in the wintry Irish Sea just now, thank you"

"I don't wish to be pedantic about it, but whales are not fish, strictly speaking, they're mammals, giving birth to calves and feeding them whale milk. They look like fish and they behave much like fish, but to be totally accurate they're not, if you get my meaning" The fact that he didn't wish to be pedantic had never stopped him before and today wasn't going to be any different.

"Listen" screeched his immediate superior "If you think for one moment that I'm in the least bit interested in the taxonomy of whales versus fish you couldn't be more wrong. Every minute you go waffling on that bloody animal up there is taking us further from land" and producing a large, wickedly sharp knife from somewhere on her capacious person she snarled "Now take this knife and climb up there and cut the rope that is connected to your fishy friend up there"

"Are you mad woman? I can't let go of the controls and go scrambling up ropes to free us, this isn't a bloody jumbo jet with an autopilot, you know. The minute I let go of the controls we'll be thrown into a nosedive and finish up in the drink, you me and the unfortunate whale, not to mention the aircraft. No, sadly it's up to you to do the scrambling bit" He looked quite self satisfied with this riposte, fortunately she couldn't see his face.

Undoing her safety belt, she hauled her not inconsiderable bulk upright and strained towards the harpoon rope connecting them to the cetacean above, complaining bitterly all the while, not being used to this type of gymnastics she tripped over the lip of the cockpit and tumbled headlong into the sea far below.

Peter gazed at her diminishing form as plummeted towards the icy water then switching on his radio he called "Nicely done there, Wally, now take us home and he hummed a tune as he went on "Oh, ain't I the Lucky Man"

Lies, Damn Lies.

"The house is on fire" screamed Grace, a very excitable three year old.

I immediately bolted from my couch of repose in front of the television and started to round up the tribe of ankle biters which had been imposed on me by their many and various owners "Just for a couple of hours" they had promised as they climbed into their cars and zoomed off about their multifarious pursuits.

Counting heads, I concluded that all were present with the exception of the excitable Grace and Max, who could be heard in the back garden giving vent to loud and delighted squeals "Look at the pretty colours of the fire"

Rushing outside I gazed in amazement as I beheld Grace and her cousin Max dancing around the merry bonfire composed of the giant dolls house which has been in our family for five generations.

"Is this the house that's on fire?" I demanded

Max, a precocious three and a half year old smiled gleefully and said "Of course, you hardly thought it was the real house?"

With a huge sigh of relief, I went back to my previously gathered clutch of bread snappers and calmed their incipient hysteria down, all the while connecting up the garden hose. I returned to the conflagration and extinguished the blaze. Sadly, all that remained of the relics of old decency were charred walls and incinerated dolls.

"How did this happen, who lit the fire, what were you two thinking?" I demanded as the miscreants stood with downcast and tear filled eyes, surrounded by their disbelieving, and in some cases admiring, siblings and cousins.

With one voice both cried "It wasn't me, he/she made me do it. I was just looking on"

"Just wait til' your parents come home; you guys are in such trouble. I guess you'll be grounded for the rest of your lives" If truth be told, I was having great trouble containing a desire to laugh out loud. I had always hated the doll's house and in my youth, it formed the backdrop to many of my childish nightmares. There was then and still is something very creepy about dolls houses.

Sadly, for me, my phobia was well known to my extended family so that when the aforesaid children's parents reappeared on the scene all the brats shouted, with total, unprompted unanimity

"Harry burned the doll's house"

Their mothers in various ways conveyed their disgust at my alleged crime, believing utterly their darling offspring and left, sadly vowing never to allow me to baby sit again.

So, a good result, all things considered?

Trains, Planes and a Leprechaun

She had missed the last train and there was only one person she could blame, herself.

"The curse of hell on this" she snarled. "If I hadn't stayed for that last donut at the Krispy Kreme place, I would've made it easily. My mother always told me my eyes were too big for my belly. Next time I'll make sure to start earlier"

Sitting disconsolately on a cold bench in an almost deserted Heuston Station she mumbled to herself

"Now I'm going to miss my plane connection for Berlin. Not to mention that I don't have any place to stay tonight and there's no money left in the budget for a hotel. Shit, shit, shit"

Suddenly, a voice spoke "Cheer up Kathleen, it could be worse. You've never died of winter yet"

"What, exactly, does that mean?" She demanded "And how could it be worse? I've missed my train, my plane and I've no place to lay my head. Define worse, please"

"Well" said the diminutive man dressed in black trousers, green jacket and slippers with the toes turned up "You might not have met me, that would really be unfortunate. My name is Brian O'Lynn and I'm king of the leprechauns, from over there in the Phoenix Park. This being Halloween, I'm going to help you out"

"Help me out?" She queried "Help me out how? And what's in it for you? My mother always told me to watch for creepy old men in railway stations, particularly late at night. I think I'll take my chances elsewhere"

338

"Oh, I can help all right" He crowed and with a snap of his finger and thumb he transported them, instantaneously, to the main Berlin railway station, just a short walk from her hotel.

"Gee thanks" she said, open mouthed with astonishment "What do I owe you?"

"Not a lot" he replied with a smarmy grin "Just give me your first born child, I have a use for her"

"Not in this lifetime" she snapped "I didn't agree to that, you should have gotten the contract sorted out before you delivered the goods. So long sucker" and she headed off towards her hotel, smiling triumphantly.

Christmas Cheer

Christmas morning dawned bright and clear, but cold. Assembling the disparate members of the family into good order the Ancient of years marshalled them all down to late mass in the parish church.

Along the way they met Mrs Murgatroyd, dressed to the height of fashion in her 'genuine' mink coat and glittery earrings and bracelets, also 'genuine.'

"Good morning Mrs Murgatroyd, fine morning for it. Happy Christmas to you and yours this blessed season" Cried the Ancient.

"Bah bloody humbug" Snarled Mrs M. "If you had the crosses to bear that I have, you wouldn't be half as cheerful as you are. My husband is lying drunk on the kitchen table, so wasted he can't even raise his head, my eldest son is in St Pats allegedly in Rehab. He's being chased by his creditors for all the money he borrowed during the boom years and he's hiding out. My youngest granddaughter is pregnant by some random go boy she found in Buck Whaleys one Friday night, she knows neither his name nor his whereabouts. My sciatica is playing up something shocking and my eyesight is failing, blessed season my arse!"

Processing rapidly onwards the family came upon a small, golden haired child, crying piteously. "What can the matter be?" Queried the Ancient.

"That old fool Santa has ruined Christmas" Lisped the waif "I clearly asked him for an Elsie doll, from the movie 'Frozen' you know, and he left me the other one, Anna. The Anna doll is lame. I can't tell all my friends that I got an Anna doll. I've already told them that Santa is bringing me the biggest bestest Elsie doll. That fat old fool must hate me. And I've been very good too, at least for the last week or two"

"Never mind" Advised the Ancient "I'm sure that Santa doesn't hate you, maybe he'd already given out his total allocation of Elsie dolls and he only had Anna's left? I'm quite sure that your Daddy will buy you an Elsie doll as soon as the shops open after Christmas"

"He bloody better" Muttered the waif.

Made in the
USA
Middletown, DE